Mary in the Bible

Jean Cantinat, C.M.

MARY

IN THE BIBLE

Translated by Paul Barrett, O.F.M.Cap.

The Newman Press • Westminster, Maryland
1965

This is a translation of *Marie dans la Bible*, first published by Éditions Xavier Mappus, Le Puy - Lyon, France, in 1963.

Nihil Obstat: Fr. Hilarius a Graigcullen, O.F.M.Cap.
            Censor theol. deput.

Imprimi Potest: Fr. Conradus a Leap, O.F.M.Cap.
            Min. Prov. Hib.
            die 10 novembris, 1964

Nihil Obstat: Rev. David Pansini, C.M.
            Censor Deputatus

Imprimatur: His Eminence, James Francis Cardinal McIntyre
            Archbishop of Los Angeles
            June 5, 1965

Contents

Mary in the Bible

Mary's Native Land

Geographical Position, and Names

PALESTINE, Mary's native country, is a narrow, relatively fertile strip of land, situated on the eastern coast of the Mediterranean and bounded on the east by the vast Syrian desert, with the Syro-Mesopotamian regions to the north and Egypt to the south. Its ancient name of Canaan is no longer used, and the title, Palestine, did not become official until the end of the second century of our era. The pagans of the Hellenistic period (300 B.C.–300 A.D.) called it Judea, that is, the country inhabited by the Jews, the descendants of the tribe of Juda. The Jews themselves called it the Promised Land, the Holy Land, and the Land of Israel. This last title, which brings to mind the patriarch Jacob whom God re-named Israel (Gen. 32:22 ff.; 35:10), is more exact than

Judea because it includes all the descendants of the twelve
tribes that sprang from Jacob and not merely those of the
tribe of Juda.[1]

Dimensions and Geography

Palestine, as such, has always been a very small country.
In Mary's time, it had almost regained its greatest political
dimensions; namely, those to which Solomon had extended it.
Yet in area it is little larger than Vermont or New Hamp-
shire; for it measures only about 125 miles from north to
south, and varies in width from 25 miles in the north to
about 87 miles in the south. But it more than makes up for
its smallness by being so picturesque, containing as it does
the surprising combination of four parallel regions, each
completely different from the others—a coastal plain traversed
by waterways that are more torrents than rivers; a chain of
hills and mountains that extends south from the mountains
of Lebanon; a deep-sunken valley through which the Jordan
flows and in which lie the Lake of Genesareth and the Dead
Sea; and finally, a high plateau, sloping down from Mount
Hermon to the east of the Jordan valley.

Climate

Palestine, lying in the sub-tropical zone, has for all practical purposes only two seasons, winter and summer; the
intervening periods are very short. Winter, from October to
March, is the rainy season, and the rains, which are torrential
and can double in volume from one year to the next, are
markedly more frequent in the north than in the south, both
at the beginning and the close of the season. Spring comes
at the end of March, when the vegetation literally springs
up, whereas in the summer, which lasts from May to Sep-

tember, everything is dried up by the great heat. In autumn and even in spring the *Khamsin*, the stifling winds from the desert, can arise and blow for days on end.

In such a land, with its four very diverse parallel regions, it is normal for climatic conditions to vary greatly from region to region even in the same season. On the coastal plain severe cold is unknown during the rainy season; and even at the height of the summer, this section often enjoys the benefit of a light sea breeze. In summer the mountain district in general has cool nights and tolerably hot days, while the northern section then has dews, mists, and cloudy condensation. But winter here is quite cold, with frost, ice and even snow in some sections. The climate is tropical in the Jordan valley, where the land drops suddenly far below the level of the Mediterranean, ranging from more than 680 feet below sea level at Lake Genesareth to a depth of over 1300 feet at the Dead Sea. In winter the temperature here is pleasant, the usual minimum reading being 59°; but in summer the heat is unbearable, for the mercury can easily climb above 120° in the shade. On the high plateau along the east bank of the Jordan the temperature, both in winter and in summer, shows the effects of the nearby Syrian desert, and there can be a difference of more than 100° between day and night.

Natural Resources

If certain biblical texts are taken literally they give the impression that Palestine was a country with abundant resources, lacking nothing (Deut. 8:7–8) and flowing with milk and honey (Exod. 3:8). However, these texts have only a relative validity; Palestine's fertility stands out in relation to the aridity of the neighboring regions. In fact, if we consider the country as a whole, we shall see that the rocky and desert regions are much more extensive than the arable lands. Even in ancient times, its resources were quite meager: grain crops and vegetables were grown on the plains, in the valleys and on the smaller parcels of land; fruit was harvested from the vine and from the olive, fig, sycamore fig, pomegranate and palm trees; there were the products of the flocks and herds that grazed right up to the edge of the desert; and fish were available from the sea and the Lake of Genesareth.

Divisions and Population

At the period we are discussing, Palestine was divided into four provinces—Judea, Samaria, Galilee and Perea. Judea, the most important of the four, was located in the south of the country and derived its name from the fact that its boundaries were approximately those of the ancient kingdom of Juda; for it lay between the sea and the Jordan, its northern border being an imaginary line drawn from the site now occupied by Tel Aviv to the mouth of the River Jaboc, while the southern frontier lay along a line drawn from Gaza to the Dead Sea. We know its principal towns— Jerusalem, the capital; the small port of Joppe; Bethlehem, the town of David; and Jericho, the pleasure resort. The inhabitants flattered themselves on being the truest descendants of ancient Israel.

To the north of Judea and less than half its size, lay Samaria, situated between the Mediterranean and the Jordan and bounded on the north by the southern slopes of Mount Carmel, by the Valley of Esdrelon and by Bethsan, the smallest of the districts in the pagan Decapolis. It prided itself on possessing Samaria-Sebaste, the ancient capital of the Northern Kingdom. The inhabitants, descended from a mixture of Israelites and Syrian colonists (721 B.C.), accepted only the Pentateuch (the first five books of the Bible) and adored God on Mount Garizim only (John 4:20). The Jews looked upon them as heretics and would not associate with them (John 4:9).

Galilee, north of Samaria, was cut off from the sea by a wide strip of Phoenician territory. Its northern frontier cut through the middle of the mountains of present-day Upper Galilee and then went across to the Jordan at Lake Huleh. The most important towns here were Sepphoris and Gischala, which are now mere memories. Only Nazareth and Cana remain, considerably grown, and the ancient cemetery of Tiberias. Galilee prided itself on its extensive tracts of arable land and on possessing Lake Genesareth, in which fish were abundant. The inhabitants were a mixture of many races, whence the name Galilee, that is, the region of the nations (*gelil haggoyim*). The territory that lay east of the Jordan and Lake Genesareth also belonged to it, at least in the reign of Herod the Great, and had many Jews among its inhabitants. This region extended from Mount Hermon to the Decapolis and from the Jordan to the desert.[2]

Perea, the least prosperous of the four provinces, was bordered on the east by the Jordan, on the north by the pagan Decapolis, and on the south by the Arab kingdom of Nabatea. The Jewish element, which predominated here, were engaged mostly in raising grain crops. They used to cross the Jordan at the Bethara ford or at that of the River Jaboc to go to the Temple in Jerusalem at the times of the great annual feasts.

It is not possible to estimate even approximately the total population of the four provinces of Palestine. The Jewish historians of that time certainly speak about the millions of pilgrims that flowed into Jerusalem for the Passover. But these numbers, which are perhaps exaggerated, also included those Jews who came from abroad, the Jews "of the diaspora," as they were then called. In fact, especially from the third century B.C. onward, very many Jews lived abroad, scattered almost everywhere in the Roman Empire (Acts 2:5 ff.).[3]

Notes

1. Cf. F. M. Abel, *Géographie de la Palestine*, 2 vols., Paris, 1933/38; L. Grollenberg, *Atlas of the Bible*, New York, Nelson, 1956; *Dictionnaire de la Bible, Supplément* (DBS), "Palestine," VI, 1960, pp. 1021–1066; M. du Buis, *Géographie de la Terre Sainte*, Paris, 1958.
2. Cf. F. M. Abel, *op. cit.*, II, Map IX and Chaps. VII–VIII.
3. Cf. DBS, article on "Dispersion."

2

Her People

ISRAEL, Mary's people, had lived in Palestine for many long centuries. Their first ancestors—Abraham, Isaac and Jacob—nomadic chieftains originating in Lower Mesopotamia, settled there about 1850 B.C. About 1700 B.C. the Israelites left Palestine for Egypt; but they returned once more about 1200 B.C. under the providential leadership of Moses and Josue after spending forty years in the desert of Sinai, where they received the Divine Law, that is, their rights and obligations as God's people. Gradually they displaced the Canaanites and Philistines; the better to do so they organized themselves into a kingdom about 1030 B.C. and were given three great kings, Saul, David and Solomon. Then, about 931 B.C., they divided into two kingdoms, that of the South, with its capital at Jerusalem, and that of the North, the capital being Samaria. Nevertheless, the Israelites as a whole enjoyed great prosperity until the two kingdoms fell, the North to the Assyrians in 722 B.C., and the South to the Babylonians in 586 B.C.

The defeat of 586 B.C. brought the Israelites' independence to an end. After their return from the long period of captivity beside the River Euphrates (586–538 B.C.), their leaders were subject to the various foreign governors appointed by the Persians, Egyptians and Syrians. Deprived of kings, independence, and political ambitions and confined to a mere part of the territory that once formed the kingdom of the South, Israel became, practically speaking, Judea. The nation really had only one possession left, the Law of their God, which, however, they had greatly neglected. Consequently, under the direction of their High Priests and scribes, they established a theocratic, or rather a hierocratic, state—Judaism.[1]

This religious transformation saved Israel from total dissolution when, from 167 B.C. on, the Greek princes of Syria tried to make it pagan. Stirred to anger, the Jews took up arms at the call of the Machabee-Hasmoneans, fought long in defense of their theocracy, and about 129 B.C. finally regained their political independence. But they lost their freedom again in 63 B.C. when the Roman legions under Pompey took possession of Jerusalem.[2]

Conquered by Rome

From 37 B.C. to 4 B.C., Herod the Great, an Arabo-Idumean, ruled the four provinces of Palestine. He had been made king of Judea by the Romans, who were the real masters of the country after Pompey's invasion in 63 B.C. His appointment prolonged, as it were, the reign of the Hasmoneans, the last Jewish dynasty, and gave the Jews the illusion of still enjoying a small part of the independence they had regained with so much difficulty a century before under the Machabee brothers. Herod carefully nurtured this illusion both by the ostentation of his reign and by the respect he showed for ancient traditions. He founded new cities— Sebaste, Caesarea, Antipatris, and Phasael; built new fortresses—Masada, Hebron, Gabaa, and Machaerus, where John the Baptist was to be imprisoned; and erected splendid buildings in the old towns, especially in Jerusalem, to which, about 19 B.C., he presented a new Temple incomparably more splendid than the old one. Yet he never won the hearts of his people, because in his private life he constantly displayed a cruelty and cynicism seldom surpassed.

Herod's death in 4 B.C. ended the unity of the kingdom, for Rome then divided the provinces among three of his sons. One of them, Archelaus, received Judea and Samaria, which, in 6 A.D., were placed under the governorship of a Roman procurator. (At the time of our Lord's public life, this procurator was, of course, Pontius Pilate.) Galilee and Perea were given to Herod's second son, Antipas, whose dealings with John the Baptist and then our Lord are well known to us all. The third son, Philip, inherited the regions lying east of the Jordan which had formed part of the province of Galilee under his father. The provinces were temporarily reunited from 41 to 46 A.D. under Agrippa I, Herod the Great's grandson; then from 44 to 66 the procuratorial system held sway over the whole country until the revolt, which was followed by the catastrophe of 70, the destruction of Jerusalem.

Religious Hierarchy

Even in the times of the Roman procurators, the civil administrators of Palestine did not by any means ignore the religious character of the people. They were careful to take account of the Mosaic Law, which, basically, was the Jews' rule of life. Thus the civil authorities allowed the guardians of the Law (the priests, scribes and men of note) to function. They confined themselves to regulating the office of the High Priest, the principal custodian of the Law, by reserving to themselves at all times the right to nominate and depose him. From the time of Herod the Great to the destruction of Jerusalem (70 A.D.), there were twenty-eight successive High Priests.

Long forgetful of their duty as religious guides, the priests neither preserved knowledge nor passed it on by instruction (Mal. 2:7 ff.). They merely saw to it that divine worship was performed in the only Temple in the nation, the great Temple in Jerusalem. To our eyes most of the rites of this worship seem very material—slaughtering, dismembering, and burning selected animals (bulls, rams, lambs, and doves), which were daily offered to God in the name of, and by, the people; storing up gifts of grain, oil and wine that were also to be offered up in one form or another; collecting the sums of money poured into the sacred treasury—dues, tithes, taxes, and spontaneous or promised gifts; carrying in the morning and evening incense, the oil and wicks for the seven-branched candlesticks, the twelve weekly loaves of bread symbolic of the twelve tribes; bringing all these into the sanctuary proper, a very large chamber containing three compartments and measuring approximately 115 by 32 feet over all.

To ensure the performance of divine services in this place of worship, the nation had about 20,000 priests, too large a number, naturally, for all of them to be employed in the Temple. Therefore only a privileged few, chosen by lot (cf. Luke 1:8) and free of any physical infirmity, took turns at officiating. Except for their leaders, who were avaricious and lived in luxury, the majority of them had only meager incomes with which to support their wives and families.

The scribes, drawn mostly from among the laymen, assumed the role of religious leaders of the people. They were apprenticed at an early age and devoted long years to the study of the Mosaic Law under the tutelage of older men whom they called Rabbis or Masters; and in their turn they taught young aspirants. They liked to remain in the porches, courts, and outer parts of the Temple in Jerusalem to instruct their fervent disciples or the admiring crowds of pilgrims (Luke 2:18); and they even went so far as to attribute doctrinal value to the least of their practices, especially in the matter of manual work, which most of them performed (cf. 2 Thess. 3:8; Acts 20:34). Indeed, they prided themselves on being the successors of Esdras the Scribe and a group apart from other men.

The men of note were those who wielded influence in the local communities and who were usually called the ancients, a title that indicated dignity rather than age. They met in council or "in sanhedrin," to settle disputes, rule on current affairs, and govern the religious congregations or synagogues. In Jerusalem, under the presidency of the reigning High Priests, they joined the leaders of the principal priestly families and the most noted scribes to form the national council or Great Sanhedrin (cf. Mk. 14:53; 15:1). All Jews, even those who lived outside Palestine, were subject to the authority of this national council (cf. Acts 9:1 f.; 28:21).

Social Classes

During the Herodian era and under the procurators, most of the people of Palestine were either poor or of very modest means. The rich, detested for their arrogance and injustice, were few in number and were found mainly among the officials of the central administration, the priestly aristocracy, the wholesale traders and the landowners. The rest of the nation, the immense majority, were engaged in agriculture, cattle-raising, or fishing. In every family the women were engaged directly in many small industries—grinding the grain into flour, baking bread, pressing oil from olives, spinning, and weaving garments. The working class was rather small and consisted only of artisans such as carpenters, blacksmiths, weavers, dyers, fullers, potters, goldsmiths, engravers, stonecutters, hairdressers, etc. (cf. Ecclus. 38:25 ff.). Slaves were still to be found in the houses of the rich. As one would expect, their lot varied greatly from one master to another (cf. Ecclus. 33:25–33); but they were usually better treated in Palestine than in the pagan world because the Mosaic Law made merciful provision for them (Exod. 21:1 ff., 26 f.; Levit. 25:46; Deut. 15:21 ff.).

Politico-Religious Parties

While the unity of the Jewish nation suffered from inequalities in the social order, it suffered still more from the politico-religious divisions among the people, divisions that had, for some time, given rise to such distinct parties as the Sadducees, the Essenes, and the Pharisees.

The Sadducees appeared for the first time about the year 153 B.C. when Jonathan, the last of the Machabee brothers and the descendant of an obscure priestly family, had himself nominated High Priest. The ancient priestly families, who had hitherto kept the high priesthood among themselves and who claimed to belong to the illustrious lineage of Sadoc (cf. 1 Kings 1:32 ff.), then banded together in opposition to Jonathan. Later on, their party, which continued to be composed mainly of priests, adapted itself to the successive political regimes in order to safeguard the members' material interests (cf. John 11:47 ff.). Ruled by unbridled greed, these Sadducees retained nothing of the Mosaic Law except a small number of external practices, and at the same time, they created around them a religious climate that was most injurious.

Reacting even more violently than the Sadducees against Jonathan's usurpation of the high priesthood, the Essenes had retreated to Qumrân in the desert, on the shores of the Dead Sea. But they soon opposed the Sadducees also, when they saw them entering into agreements with the political powers and sanctioning in practice what had at first revolted them. The Essenes lived a life of unceasing penance, study, and prayer and received as members, after a period of probation, those who came to join them. Convinced that the priestly caste was defiling God's Temple, they waited expectantly for the coming of the Messias, who would give them the signal for the annihilation of the priests. Their undeniable virtues acted as an antidote to their enemies' evil influence over the people.

The Pharisees, most influential of the three parties, included almost all the scribes. From their very founding at the beginning of the second century B.C., they had striven to guide the religious destiny of the nation. They aimed at the strict practice of the Mosaic Law, multiplied interpretations of it, represented them as ancient traditions (Mark 7:5) and very soon made them more imperative than the Law itself (Mark 7:8 ff.). They tolerated the political powers, who in turn respected them, but they vigorously opposed the Sadducees as destructive of the nation's religious heritage. Unhappily, though, their pride in their great knowledge of the Law led them to despise and regard as sinners all those who did not possess that knowledge. Worse still, they had added to the Law so many traditions of their own that even they themselves could not carry them out, and so they played the hypocrite, not practising what they preached. Shut up in their own legalistic world, in the end they were blind to the light of Christ and did all they could to turn others away from Him (Matt. 15:12–14).[3] Nevertheless, not all the Pharisees were affected by this spirit of hypocrisy; there were some who displayed admirable goodness of life (John 9:16; Acts 15:5). Not to recognize this would be to doubt the testimony that St. Paul, after his conversion, gave about his life as a Pharisee (Phil. 3:6; 1 Tim. 1:13).

Notes

1. M. J. Lagrange, Le Judaïsme avant Jésus-Christ, Paris, 1931, p. 33 ff., 608.

2. F. M. Abel, Histoire de la Palestine, I, Paris, 1952; F. M. Abel and J. Starcky, Les Livres des Maccabées, Paris, 1961; Daniel-Rops, Daily Life in the Time of Jesus, tr. by P. O'Brian (New York, Hawthorn, 1962) p. 48 ff.

3. For more on the three parties see Lagrange, op. cit., pp. 268–337; J. Bonsirven, Le Judaïsme Palestinien au temps de Jésus-Christ, Paris, I (1935), pp. 41–70; J. T. Milik, Dix ans de découvertes dans le désert de Juda, Paris, 1957 (tr. Illinois: Allenson, 1959); Bible et Terre Sainte, no. 4, July, 1957; Millar Burrows, The Dead Sea Scrolls, Viking, New York, 1955; New Light on the Dead Sea Scrolls (Viking, New York, 1957).

3

Her Religion

The Holy Books

IN THE LONG COURSE of its history Israel had been enriched with the extensive religious literature which we call the Old Testament; in it were set down the traditions of its patriarchs, the precepts of its lawmakers, the annals or chronicles of its leaders, kings and heroes, the oracles of its great prophets, the songs of its psalmists, and the maxims or sayings of its moralists.

For practical reasons, as for example ease of handling in private or public reading, the Jews divided their sacred literature into three sections—the Law (of Moses) or the *Torah*, which contained the Pentateuch or first five books of the Bible; the Prophets or *Nebiim*, made up of more than twenty books, six of which were historical rather than prophetical;

the Writings (*Hagiographa*) or *Kethubim* composed of all the other books, at least fifteen in number. But often, for the sake of brevity, the whole collection was called "the Law and the Prophets" (Matt. 5:17).

The Jews believed that all these books were divinely inspired and therefore sacred, as is evident from many biblical texts (e.g., 1 Mach. 12:9; 2 Mach. 2:15; 2 Tim. 3:18; 2 Pet. 1:20f.), the letter of Pseudo-Aristeas, a work of the Jewish historian, Flavius Josephus (*Contra Apion*, I, 8), and the apocryphal *Apocalypse of Esdras* (4 Esd. 14:23 ff.).[1]

Principal Beliefs

Every Jew of Mary's time who accepted this sacred literature and was instructed in it at home, in the Temple or the synagogue, possessed a large number of religious beliefs.

Above all, he believed in the existence of the one God, the Creator of the universe. Every day he expressed his belief in monotheism (Deut. 6:4) and declared that he was ready to defend it at the cost of his life, as his ancestors had done during the insurrection of the Machabees (167–164 B.C.). He did not waver at the idea of God's transcendence but rather emphasized it, to judge by the care he took to use roundabout phrases and abstract terms in speaking of God. He knew all God's attributes, including His mercy and fatherhood, but he was more inclined to dwell on those that inspired in him a certain reserve; and his manner of obeying the laws set down in the sacred books, reflected this attitude; he was so fearful of violating the letter of these laws that he sometimes failed to see their spirit.

He believed also in the world of spirits, in angels and devils, for no one can listen long to readings from the Bible without learning about this subject. The immense number of angels, their hierarchy, their spiritual nature, their role

as servants in the heavenly courts and as messengers to men—
all this was revealed to him with special precision in the
Books of Job (1:6 ff.), Tobias (12:15 ff.) and Daniel (7:10;
12:1). In like manner, he was taught about the evil powers
of the devils and particularly of their leader, Satan, who
brought sin and death into the world (Job 1:6 ff.; 2:1 ff.;
Tob. 8 ff.; Wisd. 2:24).

The good Jew of this era was more fortunate than his
ancestors; unlike them, he was not ignorant of the fate that
awaited him after death. He did not look upon the life
beyond the grave as a more or less lethargic state of existence
in *sheol,* a dark, dusty region in the subterranean world. With
Daniel, the Machabean martyrs, and the author of the Book
of Wisdom, he knew that when the just man died he received
a happy eternal reward and that on the last Day of Yahweh
his body would rise again in glory.

Yet he hoped that before he himself died he would see
the coming of the Messias, God's extraordinary envoy, of
whom the prophets spoke. He fervently hoped to have a
part in the ideal kingdom which the Messias was to establish,
and the obstacles that stood in the way only fanned his ardor.
Moreover, all around him he heard different opinions about
what the Messias would be and about the nature and duration
of his work. While no one even dreamed of a divine Being,
many thought that the Messias would be a king like David,
with a politico-religious program for establishing a kingdom
in which the Chosen People's glory and temporal happiness
would play at least as big a part as the worship of God's
sovereignty.

Main Religious Practices of Worship

The daily service in the Temple consisted of two holo-
causts, one in the morning and the other in the afternoon

(Exod. 29:38 ff.; Num. 28:2 ff.). To acknowledge God's sovereignty over all, a freshly killed lamb, free from blemish, was burned whole on an immense altar in the Court of the Priests (2 Kings 16:15)[2] facing the sanctuary; a small amount of flour soaked in oil was also offered and a small quantity of wine poured out. Only at the morning sacrifice did the priest go into the section of the sanctuary next to the Holy of Holies to place the burning coals and incense on the altar of incense. On feast days the number of offerings was increased, and at certain times a total of two bulls, a ram, and seven lambs were burned at one sacrifice (Num. 28:11 ff.).

Obviously, only those who lived nearby and had sufficient free time, were able to attend the daily services in the Temple; and they had to do so from a distance since they were allowed to enter only as far as the courts outside the Court of the Priests. Others waited until the great yearly feasts came around—in the spring, the Passover, commemorating the freeing of the Israelites thirteen centuries before; Pentecost, or the harvest festival; and the Feast of Tabernacles, in the autumn, recalling the sojourn in the desert of Sinai, and celebrating the grape harvest (Lev. 23: 1 ff.). On these occasions the roads of Palestine were crowded with pilgrims, singing as they went up to the capital and its Temple. When they arrived, they intoned the well-known psalm: "I rejoiced because they said to me, 'We will go up to the house of the Lord.' And now we have set foot within your gates, O Jerusalem . . ." (Ps. 121[122]:1–2). Then they pitched their tents on the hills around the city before thronging down into the immense courts of the sacred enclosure. Every week, for twenty-four hours, from Friday to Saturday evening, the whole Jewish people devoted themselves to another form of divine worship by observing the Sabbath (Exod. 31:13 ff.), the day of rest, in honor of God and in commemoration of the

seventh day of Creation. On this day all bodily activity and
even all journeys of any length were forbidden; and the
Jews prayed, meditated, read their sacred books and heard
them explained. Those who lived in Jerusalem went to the
Temple or to one of the innumerable synagogues in the city,
while those who lived elsewhere went to their local synagogues. The service in the synagogue began with the
prayer *Shema Israel*, the profession of faith in one God
(Deut. 6:4–9; 11:13–21; Num. 15:37–41), followed by
the reading and translation of an inspired text, which a
chosen speaker then expounded (Luke 4:16 ff.; Acts 13:15).
The service closed with another prayer, one of blessing, and
the final *Amen*. The Gospel tells us of the Holy Family's
perfect fidelity to this type of religious observance (Luke
4:16).

Finally, once every year the whole nation again paid
homage to its God by keeping a rigorous fast for twenty-four
hours, the only fast prescribed by the Law (Lev. 16:31),
to be observed on the Day of Atonement, *Yom Kippur*, a
short while before the Feast of Tabernacles in the autumn.
This was the only day in the year when the High Priest
could enter the Holy of Holies, the inner part of the sanctuary. Then, too, the people were sprinkled with the blood
of a he-goat, and they freed themselves from their sins by
sending out into the desert another he-goat, the scapegoat,
upon which the sins of every Jew were laid.[3]

Personal and Family Devotions

The principal religious functions were really only the
more solemn manifestations of a faith that impregnated
every action of the good Jew's life, and were not in any
way isolated incidents or strange interludes in a life otherwise
entirely divorced from God. From morning to night, from

one end of the year to the other, the Jewish people led a life of religion, because God's law, or at least what they were taught to revere as His law, regulated both their work and their leisure. St. Paul, the former scribe, was to transpose this spirit of religion to Christianity when he wrote to the Corinthians: "Therefore, whether you eat or drink, or do anything else, do all for the glory of God" (1 Cor. 10:31).

Every Jew, as soon as he reached religious maturity, at about the age of thirteen, was bound to recite many prayers aloud several times a day. And although only the boys and men were bound by this regulation, the girls and women did not dispense themselves from it. When praying, the Jew stood, turned toward Jerusalem, and lifted his arms to heaven. His head was covered with his *talith,* a shawl with fringes and tassels on it, and on his forehead and left arm he wore the *tephillim* or phylacteries, small cases containing sacred texts. The times of prayer were, in practice, fixed, for they coincided with the hours of sacrifice in the Temple and with meal times. The principal prayer was once more the *Shema Israel:* "Hear, O Israel! The Lord is our God, the Lord alone! Therefore, you shall love the Lord, your God, with all your heart, and with all your soul, and with all your strength. Take to heart these words . . ." (Deut. 6:4 ff.).

To keep his soul in a spirit of prayer and to remind him of the Lord's commandments, the Jew also placed phylacteries at the entrance to his house and wore fringes on the edges of his garments (Num. 15:38 ff.; Matt. 9:20, 23:5), practised numerous ablutions that marked him off from profane men (Mark 7:1 ff.; Luke 7:44; Matt. 23:25), kept many fasts (Luke 5:33; 18:12), gave alms (Matt. 6:1 ff.; Luke 21:1 ff.), and ate only cold food on the Sabbath day.

In addition, it was every father's duty to teach his sons the commandments of God, to tell them the story of God's ancient interventions on behalf of the Jewish nation, and explain to them the religious significance of the feasts of the year (Exod. 13:8; Deut. 4:10; 6:7; 11:19; Prov. 4:1; 22:6 etc.).

Obviously, this intense religious atmosphere did not have the same effect on all those who received the benefit of it. Some, such as the materialistic Sadducees or the less generous of the Pharisees, profited less by it; but others, such as the aged Simeon, Anna the prophetess, the parents of St. John the Baptist, St. Joseph, and still more, Mary, found in it the way to very high sanctity.

Notes

1. Cf. Robert-Feuillet, *Introduction à la Bible*, Paris, 1959, p. 6 ff.
2. Cf. R. de Vaux, *Les Institutions de l'Ancien Testament*, Paris, II, 285.
3. Cf. R. de Vaux, *op. cit.*, II, 415 ff.

4

The Jewish Woman of Mary's Day

The Young Girl

AT THE TIME about which we are speaking, as in former ages, the birth of a daughter was a happy event in the Jewish family; the dream of a numerous posterity was still vivid in the Jewish heart, and a large family was regarded as a sign of God's blessing, a pledge of prosperity and of survival in this world (Deut. 21:18; Ps. 128:1). Sterility was therefore considered a trial, a punishment even (Luke 1:25). It is true that sons were preferred to daughters, but this was only because girls left the family when they married and therefore did not perpetuate the line or the family name and fortune.

The mother had exclusive care of her daughter until the day of the girl's espousals; but the father was not therefore unconcerned about the child. He saw to it that she would not make him "a laughing-stock to (his) enemies, a byword in the city, and a reproach among the people" (cf. Ecclus. 42:9 ff.). As soon as the child was born, the mother gave her a name which was inspired by the circumstances of her birth or conception, or taken from the world of plants and animals, or else made up of an abstract word and a shortened form of God's name, Elohim or Yahweh. For hygienic reasons, to avoid the often fatal dysentery caused by goat's milk, the mother herself nursed the baby for two or three years. She undertook, with a firm hand, the child's religious and moral formation, (Prov. 13:24; 22:15; Eccli. 35:1 ff.) but she also allowed her to spend most of her free time playing with other children (Matt. 11:16 f.). The mother, of course, was aware that many of the traditional obligations did not bind girls but she knew also that her daughter would one day have to educate her own children and even encourage her own husband in the practice of his religion. So the mother was diligent in ensuring that her daughter received a thorough religious education. As soon as the child was old enough, the mother enlisted her aid in all household tasks and even, when necessary, in work in the fields, teaching her how to keep house efficiently and preparing her for her approaching role as wife and mother.

The worst misfortune that could befall a young girl then was to be sold by her father as a slave because he was hard-pressed for money (Lev. 25:42 ff.; 27:3). On the other hand, the best fate that could befall her, according to the opinion of the day, was to be an only child so that she could eventually inherit the family possessions (Num. 27:9; 36: 2 ff.), and be much sought after by suitors. According to the apocryphal writings, this was the case with Mary.

Wife and Mother

When she reached marrying age, about her thirteenth year, the young Jewish girl soon received a proposal of marriage. The first step was taken by the young man's father or, more rarely, by the young man himself, who approached the girl's parents and suggested a certain sum of money, called the *mohar*, to be given by way of compensation to the family. When everything had been arranged—all without consulting the girl herself—gifts were added to the *mohar* as a sign of gratitude to the family for acceding to the suitor's request. From that moment on, the young man and the girl were betrothed and were bound by juridical ties analogous to those of marriage. After an interval of varying length, the actual wedding ceremony took place, consisting essentially of installing the bride in the groom's house. All the rest, including the procession with singing, music and lights from the bride's house to that of the groom, and the ensuing days of festivity, was simply so much display.

Even after her marriage the young bride was still regarded as a minor. She belonged to her husband now just as she had formerly belonged to her father; her emancipation from the one only meant her becoming subject to the other. The validity of any vows or pledges she might make always depended upon her husband's consent; and her hopes of being a rich heiress were now even dimmer than before her marriage. Yet her position was less precarious than before because she could no longer be sold or treated as a slave (Deut. 21:14; Exod. 21:7); and she had more protection under the Law (Deut. 21:13 ff.). Since in most cases the family into which the girl married was in modest circumstances, she had to do her share of the work. Not only was she expected to bear many children, but she also had to be diligent in performing all the usual household tasks. Yet these duties were the basic elements of her happiness. The birth of her children, especially of her sons, brought her an increase in consideration and affection, for from then on she was regarded as the obvious intermediary of God's blessing. Then, too, her motherhood gave her added guarantees for the future since the Law commanded that children, even when grown up, should honor their mother as much as their father (Lev. 19:3; Exod. 20:12). Her diligence at work, her household skills and her other virtues helped to win her husband's heart; and we can sense in the Scriptures the tenderness with which the husband surrounded his wife because of the sterling qualities she displayed (Prov. 31:10 ff.; Ecclus. 26:1 ff.) and the care she took of the children.

As we have seen, it was she who took almost exclusive charge of her daughters until they were married; but her sons were under her direct care only during their early years, after which the father took them in hand to educate them, train them in his trade or profession, give them religious instruction, and thus prepare them to become, at about thirteen years of age, full-fledged subjects of the Law. Yet it goes without saying that the mother's influence continued to affect the sons indirectly in a thousand and one ways.

The Divorcée and the Widow

Without great risk of error, we can state that, generally speaking, the Jewish husband not only loved his wife but also treated her as an equal.[1] However, we have to admit that there must have been frequent exceptions, for human passions are the same in all ages, and the provisions of law in those days gave husbands great facilities for satisfying those passions.

Although the wife was bound to absolute fidelity to her husband under penalty of death, he was never held guilty of adultery so far as she was concerned (Exod. 20:14; Deut. 5:18; 22:23). In addition to his wife, a rich husband could have other women, either as wives properly so called, as concubines, or as slaves.[2] The man who was too poor to practice this type of polygamy could have recourse to taking several wives in succession by using the right of dismissal (Deut. 24:1). A whole school of scribes, the disciples of Hillel, authorized a husband to send away as many wives as he wished and for any reason at all (Matt. 19:1 ff.; Ecclus. 25:26). When we read certain Biblical exhortations, we see that this authorization was by no means a dead letter and that it was used very lightly at times (Mal. 2:14 ff.; Prov. 5:18; Ecclus. 7:28; 25:36).

The wife who was dismissed received a bill of divorce, signed before witnesses (Deut. 24:1 f.; Isa. 50:1; Jer. 3:8), and from then on she was free in the eyes of society and could, if the circumstances were favorable, enter another marriage without running the risk of being branded an adulteress.[3] In practice, however, when a woman was divorced she was often too old to have a chance of marrying again. So with only her personal effects in her possession, she returned to her father's house where, with rare exceptions, she was received as a mere servant or even a slave (Lev. 19:29; 21:14; Ecclus. 33:25 ff.).

Frequently a widow was in a similar or even worse position than a divorcée. Unless she had children or, in accordance with the levirate law, was taken as a wife by her brother-in-law (levir), her dead husband's brother (Deut. 25:5 ff.), she too returned to her father's house. If she had young children to take care of, she did not have a moment's rest and became an easy prey to exploitation (Matt. 23:14)—

a state of affairs eloquently proved by the many interventions of the religious laws on behalf of widows (Deut. 24:17 ff.). In fact, Scripture depicts widows and orphans as symbols of misery (Ps. 109:9; Jer. 18:21; James 1:27). Only the widow who, like Judith (8:7), possessed great riches or whose sons could take care of her, escaped this sad fate.[4]

God's Plan

Although in practice Jewish women were obviously in a subordinate position, theoretically they enjoyed a completely different status. But they did not possess many of the elements needed for discovering this in their own religious law. Today, however, we know the facts of the matter.

The passages in Genesis about Creation suggest that woman is really equal to man and that, in a way, the one is the complement of the other. This equality is evident from God's decision to give man a helper like himself, someone to be paired with him; from the fact that man could not find a helper of this kind among the animals that paraded before him; and from his exclamation upon seeing the first woman: "She . . . is bone of my bone, and flesh of my flesh; she shall be called Ishah (woman), for from man (Ish) she has been taken" (Gen. 2:23). The reciprocal function of man and woman can be seen from the order in which they were created, first the man and then the woman (1 Tim. 2:13); from the role of helper assigned to the woman (1 Cor. 11:8–9); from the name that Adam gave his partner, for we must not forget that, in the ancient eastern world, to name something implied domination over it; and from the man's initiative in leaving his parents in order to cleave to his wife (Gen. 2:18–25). All of this leads us to believe that "even in the state of original justice, man would have had authority in marriage" (A. M. Henry). But "he should not become

vain over a role that has been given him by God, any more
than he can resign that role at will. It is none of his doing
that he is a man and that God has ordained that he has
one kind of duty in marriage while the woman has another.
Although the duties are different, the persons are equal"
(*Idem.*: cf. 1 Cor. 11:12; Gen. 1:27).[5]

The Mosaic Law confirmed this teaching in a concrete
manner. Making the necessary allowances, the Law subjected
the woman to the same moral obligations as the man, bound
her to the same practice of religion, and accorded her rights
of the same kind. It recalled the roles of first importance
that she played in many circumstances and compared her
duty in matrimony to that of the nation, God's spouse or
betrothed.[6]

Notes

1. Cf. R. de Vaux, *op. cit.*, I, 68.
2. The growth of poverty after the Babylonian Captivity (586–538 B.C.)
   made simultaneous polygamy rare and changed it into successive
   polygamy: cf. DBS, article on "Mariage," p. 923.
3. A bill of divorce, dating from the second century A.D., was discovered
   in the caves of Murabba'at, near the Dead Sea: cf. *Revue Biblique*
   (RB), 1961, p. 418; R. de Vaux, *op. cit.*, I, 60.
4. On the status of Jewish women in this era, cf. *Cahiers du Clergé Rural*,
   March–April, 1958, pp. 133–144; *Masses ouvrières*, April, 1956,
   p. 10 ff.; 1958, p. 13 ff.; *Cahiers Marials*, Jan.–Feb., 1959; DBS, article
   on "Mariage"; R. de Vaux, *op. cit.*, I (Paris, 1957), p. 39 ff.
5. Cf. *Lumière et Vie*, no. 43, July–Aug., 1959, *Conception chrétienne
   de la femme*, p. 100 ff.
6. Cf. *Cahiers du Clergé Rural*, March–April, 1958, p. 141 ff.; *La Vie
   Catholique*, Oct. 31–Nov. 6, 1962, p. 15; *Lumière et Vie*, no. 43,
   p. 9, 55 ff.

Mary Prefigured in the Bible

Preparations for Mary's Coming

T HE WHOLE BIBLE is concerned with God's plan of redemption, the Old Testament with the preparations for it and the New with its realization and happy results. Therefore, since Mary occupies such a pre-eminent place in the fulfillment of the divine plan, we expect "to discover in the Old Testament a prediction, or at least a prefiguring, of her coming, her virtues and her mission."[1]

The Church, through her liturgists, Fathers and theologians, has encouraged this expectation and, in a way, has sketched out the path of discovery. In fact, she unceasingly uses the texts of the Old Testament to speak about Mary and to sing her glory, and shows that Mary was predicted and prefigured there by the inspired authors in such a way that her life and actions began before her actual appearance on the historical scene.[2]

Before we examine this matter, however summarily, we must make one observation which will allow us to clarify the meaning of the Bible's preparation for Mary:

After all, the figures and even the explicit predictions in the Old Testament are only surface phenomena whereas the real preparation for the Messias and for Mary was done in the depths (of men's hearts). Before the necessarily imperfect images of Him and her who were to come could be sketched in outline, their ways had to be prepared for them by imparting to men's minds and hearts an appreciation of God, morality, the value of the soul and supernatural things. If this concrete preparation had not been done, would Christ and Mary have been understood when they came? Would their coming have even been possible? In short, the entire Old Testament bore witness to them by gradually outlining their virtues. When Jesus would appear, He would gather together in Himself, and at the same time surpass, all of the various predicted elements. And, due proportion being guarded, we can say the same about the Queen of the Patriarchs and Prophets.[3]

Mary Directly Foretold in the Bible

The biblical passages that, in the literal sense, prophesy Mary's role and privileges are very few in number. In the opinion of exegetes, there are only two or three such passages, the first being in the Book of Isaias (7:14), the second in the Book of Michea (5:2–3a), and the third—which is far from being as cogent as the other two, in Genesis (3:15).

The text from Isaias (7:14) takes us to the city of Jerusalem in 736 B.C., when it was being threatened by an invasion from two neighboring states. The passage in which the text occurs, describes how the king of Juda, eager to extricate himself from the situation, wanted to call upon the

Assyrian armies to help him. But the prophet Isaias besought
the monarch to trust in God rather than in human strength,
and proposed to perform a miracle to confirm his promise of
God's help. The Scripture goes on to relate that, when the
king refused the prophet's proposal, Isaias immediately replied by foretelling the devastation that would occur and by
prophesying the survival of the royal line. He said: "The Lord
himself will give you a sign. Behold: the girl is with child
and is going to give birth to a son whom she shall call Emmanuel (God with us). . . . Yahweh shall bring upon you,
and upon your people . . . days such as have not come since
the separation of Ephraim and Juda. . . . For the whole
land shall become briers and thorns" (7:14,17,24b*).[4]

St. Matthew's Gospel sees the virginal birth of Christ,
the true Emmanuel (God with us: Matt. 1:23), as the
fulfillment of the consoling part of this text from Isaias; and
the whole of Christian tradition also acknowledges it as a
veiled announcement of the Lord's birth. The solemnity
of the prophecy, the manner of describing the young mother
(a description which the ancient Greek translation stresses
by speaking of a "virgin" and not just a girl), the symbolic
name given to the child—all this effectively demonstrates
that there is question here of a decisive intervention by God
dealing with the messianic kingdom which the text goes on
to evoke so clearly and insistently (Isa. 9:1–6; 11:1–9).[5] Yet
some authors do not fully accept these conclusions. While
admitting that the prophecy in question is truly messianic,
they believe that, primarily, it directly foretells only the
approaching birth of a child, either to the king or the
prophet.[6]

The text in the Book of Michea (5:1–2a) places us
in the presence of the devastation foretold by Isaias, which
came to pass in 701 B.C. The Assyrian troops who had been

called in to help in 736 B.C. now returned to the land of Juda, but this time as conquerors laying waste everything in their path. Before they were providentially and mysteriously defeated (cf. Isa. 37:36 ff.), they demanded the surrender of Jerusalem (cf. Isa. 36:16 ff.); whereupon the prophet Michea intervened to hearten the besieged citizens by predicting the future glory of their royal dynasty, now menaced so seriously by the Assyrian invaders. This is what the prophet said: "From you (Bethlehem-Ephrata) shall be born to me he who is to reign over Israel; his origins go back . . . to the ancient days (of the Davidic dynasty). . . . Yahweh . . . shall abandon (His people) until the time when she who is to give birth shall have given birth . . ." (5:1–2a*). This veiled allusion to Isaias's prophecy (7:14) implied that the birth of the Savior-King was to be miraculous, and thus implicitly confirms the interpretation favoring the virginal conception. But only the events themselves would make everything clear.

The text in Genesis (3:15) contains the sentence passed on the Serpent-tempter in the earthly paradise after the fall of our first parents: "I will put enmity between you and the woman, between your seed and her seed. He shall crush your head, and you shall lie in wait for his heel."

In the sentence passed, the tempter's punishment was also a promise of re-instatement for man, the first tidings of salvation, the Protoevangelium. The Hebrew text attributes the promised victory to the woman's "seed" (zera') in general. But the Greek translation, by using the masculine (autos) instead of the neuter (auto) found in the Hebrew, attributes the victory to one of the woman's sons: hence the messianic interpretation that sees Christ the Savior as this son. The Greek translation also gives Mary, the Mother of the Savior, a part in the prophesied victory; and the Latin translation, by changing the Hebrew neuter and the Greek masculine into the feminine (*ipsa conteret*), practically attributes the victory to the woman, that is, to the Mother of the Savior. It is upon this Latin translation, which must be taken with caution, that the Marian interpretations of the text are based. However, these interpretations are equally founded on the acknowledged parallel between Eve and Mary.[7]

Mary Prefigured in the Bible

Although, as we saw, texts dealing directly with Mary are very rare in the Old Testament, the same is not true of passages applied to her symbolically or figuratively, in an accommodated or "typical" sense. The list of these is a long one, and to draw it up in full would require a re-reading of many patristic, liturgical and theological documents. In fact, anthologies and abstracts of anthologies of the pertinent texts have been compiled.[8] Because of the progress that has been made in exegesis, we must exercise greater discretion and prudence in using such texts. Here we shall merely point out the more common ones.

Images of Mary's greatness or beneficence have been readily seen in *the realities of the physical world;* for example in the stars, especially the morning star; in the dawn, herald of the full light of day; in the rainbow, a sign of relief and calm; in the clouds and the earth, the elements of fruitfulness.[9] And she has been seen prefigured in *the events and scenes of sacred history:* for example, in the earthly paradise, a happy fertile land; in Noe's ark, containing a new humanity; in Jacob's ladder, where heaven and earth meet; in the burning bush, indestructible and a witness to God's presence; in Gedeon's fleece, covered with heavenly dew.[10]

The *ancient Hebrew liturgy* has suggested many symbols of Mary. She has been seen as the new Jerusalem in which God resides and which He protects; as the sanctuary of the Most High; as the holy Ark which contains the Law-giver Himself; as the golden vessel filled with heavenly manna; as the closed door through which God alone has passed.[11] She has been seen as symbolized by *the holy women* who played important roles in biblical history: she is the new Eve, victorious over the devil, and the source of true life; another Sara, giving the world the promised Son; a second Debbora, leading her people to victory; another Judith noted for her virtues, liberator of Israel, and laden with honors; an Esther, whose courage and piety overcome evil.[12]

But symbols of Mary have been seen especially in *metaphorical personifications*, as in the divine Wisdom of the Sapiential Books. It is a Wisdom that was present, as was Mary, in the thought of God the Creator of the world; that is the object of His special love; that co-operates in His work and wishes to communicate the divine gifts to all men (Prov. 8; Ecclus. 24). Mary has also been seen symbolized by Israel, the nation that was the beloved spouse of Yahweh, of which the prophets speak (Os. 1–3, etc.) and the Canticle of Canticles sings. Everything praiseworthy in Yahweh's nation-spouse has been attributed to Mary too—its beauty, its search for the beloved spouse (Cant. 2:1 f.; 4:7; etc.), even its pain in time of suffering: "Come, all you who pass by the way, look and see whether there is any suffering like my suffering" (Lament. 1:12).[13]

Notes

1. A. Robert, *Maria, Etudes sur la Sainte Vierge*, I, (Paris, 1948) p. 23.
2. Cf. G. Démaret, *Marie de qui est né Jésus*, I (Paris, 1937), p. 199.

3. A. Robert, *loc. cit.*, p. 39; cf. *Evangéliser*, March–April, 1954; *Caté-chiser*, no. 21, *A la découverte de l'Ancien Testament*, by A. Gelin.
4. *Translator's note:* When a biblical reference is marked with an aster-isk, it means that I have followed the French version used by the author, and not the Confraternity Edition, as elsewhere.
5. Cf. A. Robert, *ibid.*, p. 36 ff; A. Feuillet, in *Maria*, vol. 6, p. 25; DBS, article on "Isaïe," p. 657 f.
6. Cf. *Bible de Jérusalem*, ed. 1956, p. 996, note e.
7. Cf. A. Robert, *ibid.*, p. 34 ff.; R. de Vaux, *La Genèse*, Paris, 1951, p. 48 f.; *Bible de Jérusalem*, p. 11.
8. Cf. G. Démaret, *op. cit.*; L. Dumeste, *Notre-Dame d'Israël* (Paris, 1936), pp. 35–65; A. Robert, *ibid.*, pp. 26–34.
9. Cf. Ps. 8:4; 19:2; Ecclus. 50:6; Cant. 6:10; Gen. 9:12 ff.; 1 Kings 18:41 ff.; Deut. 8:7; Ps. 85:13, etc.
10. Cf. Gen. 2:8 f.; 6:18; 9:18 f.; 28:12; Exod. 3:2; Judges 6:36 ff.
11. Cf. Ps. 87; 127; 147; Deut. 12:5; Exod. 40:20; 16:33 f.; Ezech. 44:1 f.
12. Cf. Gen. 3:15; 17:15 ff.; Judges 4–5; Jud. 10–16; Esther 5:1 ff.; 14–15. It has been truly said that the Gospel accounts of Christ's infancy fill in and complete many former narratives; Laurentin, *Struc-ture et Théologie de Luc*, I–II, Paris, 1957; J. Troadec, *Cahiers Evan-gile*, no. 13, *La Bible et la Vierge*, Paris, 1954, p. 25 ff.
13. For the meaning of the Canticle of Canticles, cf. A. Robert, *ibid.*, p. 31 ff.; *Bible de Jérusalem*, p. 856 f.

6

Her Descent from David

Genealogies in Ancient Israel

IN ANCIENT ISRAEL genealogies were held in high esteem, as is evident from many biblical documents—from Genesis (5:10; 25; 36; 46) to the First Book of Machabees (2:1), through Numbers (1–3:26), Esdras (2), Nehemias (7:6 ff.), Chronicles (1:1–4; 7–8) and even Ruth (4:18 ff.). This was due to the conviction that the right to share in the messianic benefits depended upon the authenticity of one's claim to membership in one of the twelve tribes of Israel. And those who were descended from David were more interested in the matter than anyone else, because it was the common belief that the Fulfiller of Promises, the Messias-Savior of Israel, was to come from the line of David.

There was a whole special type of literature, made up

of genealogical lists and characterized especially by the broad schematic design of the generations quoted and by the half-legal, half-natural meaning given to the term "to beget" (*hôlid*).

The Gospel Genealogies

The two genealogies handed down to us in the Gospels of St. Matthew and St. Luke must be read in the light of this social atmosphere and literary type. The one in St. Matthew (1:1–17) is in descending order, beginning with Abraham (1:2), the depository of the oldest messianic promises, and King David (1:6), the most illlustrious ancestor of the Messias. The genealogy names St. Joseph as the last link in the chain and ends with Jesus, "who is called the Messias" (1:16*). The pattern, emphasized by the Evangelist himself (1:17), is apparent and consists of three series of fourteen names each. The object of the list, which is less evident, is to show that Jesus, the heir of the promises made to the Chosen People's first patriarch, is truly the Messias, the New David, who will usher in the ancient promises by coming to establish the expected kingdom. This aim fits in with that of the whole first Gospel, which is precisely to prove how Jesus's person and work fulfill completely the predictions of the Law and the Prophets.[1]

The genealogy in the third Gospel (Luke 3:23–38) also mentions Abraham and David but it is in ascending order, going from Jesus, son of Joseph (3:23), to Adam, the father of mankind (3:38). It, too, has a marked pattern, consisting of eleven groups of seven generations each. In this way it seeks to establish that Jesus completes not only the history of the Chosen People but also that of all men, an aim that corresponds very closely to the universalist theme of the whole third Gospel; for St. Luke is, in fact, intent on showing, among other things, that Jesus is the Savior of the world.[2]

Mary and the Gospel Genealogies

At first it is rather surprising to find that both these genealogies are of St. Joseph and not of Mary. We get the impression that we are faced with a contradiction because, on the one hand, the Evangelists tell us clearly that St. Joseph was only the *legal* father of Jesus (Matt. 1:18 ff.; Luke 1:27; 2:5), while on the other hand they appeal to the genealogies, which deal with *Joseph's* lineage alone, to prove that Jesus was descended from David. Our surprise disappears, however, when we learn that in the eyes of the ancient Jews legal paternity, as a result of adoption or the levirate law, was of sovereign importance and conferred all hereditary rights on the child.[3] In the present case, therefore, since Joseph truly belonged to the royal, messianic line, as his genealogy proves, he transmitted to Jesus the rights of the royal lineage by the mere fact that he was His legal father.

This same law of legal paternity also gives us the key to another difficulty encountered in the Gospel genealogies. Seventeen of the nineteen names between David and St. Joseph are different in the two lists, notably the two names given to Joseph's father—Jacob in one list (Matt. 1:16) and Heli in the other (Luke 3:23). The divergence can be explained, however, "either by the fact that (St.) Matthew preferred to give the dynastic succession rather than the natural line, or by the equivalence set up between legal descent (through adoption or the levirate law) and natural descent" (P. Benoit).

Furthermore, in comparatively recent times and certainly not before the sixteenth century, one opinion held that St.

Matthew was giving St. Joseph's genealogy while St. Luke was giving Mary's. But this theory disregarded ancient Jewish customs and was based on an incorrect reading of a phrase in St. Luke's genealogy. Instead of: "Jesus . . . being—as was supposed—the son of Joseph, the son of Heli . . . ," the proponents of the theory read: "Jesus . . . being the son of Heli, although he was thought to be the son of Joseph. . . ." And they took Heli to be a shortened form of Eliachim or Joachim, and identified him with Joachim, Mary's father. This opinion, however, no longer has the support of reputable authors.[4]

Mary's Descent from David

Because Mary is not included in the two genealogies, it does not necessarily follow that she did not belong to the family of David. There are other Gospel texts that deal with this question, and we must consider them before reaching any conclusion.

In the account of the Annunciation we read: "The angel Gabriel was sent . . . to a virgin betrothed to a man named Joseph, of the house of David, and the virgin's name was Mary" (Luke 1:26–27). Apparently only *Joseph's* Davidic descent is mentioned here because, among other reasons, the words "of the house of David," seem to apply most naturally to him since they come immediately after his name. Nevertheless, it is not impossible that the Evangelist was thinking more of Mary's descent than of Joseph's because the whole passage is concerned with her.

When the angel Gabriel announced to Mary that God would give her Son the throne of David His father (Luke 1:32), he did not affirm her Davidic descent; nor did Zachary, when he blessed God for having raised up a power for salvation in the house of David His servant through the conception of Jesus (Luke 1:69). Perhaps both the angel and

Zachary were thinking only of St. Joseph's legal paternity, with which the genealogical lists are concerned. And the same is true of St. Paul and the Apocalypse when speaking of Jesus: "(God's) Son who was born to him according to the flesh of the offspring of David . . ." (Rom. 1:3), and "he who has the key of David" (Apoc. 3:7; 5:5; 22:16).

During the census of Quirinius, mentioned by St. Luke in connection with the birth of Jesus (2:1 ff.), all the inhabitants of Palestine went to be enrolled in their town of origin. St. Joseph left Nazareth for Bethlehem, the town of David, "because he was of the house and family of David . . . , together with Mary his espoused wife, who was with child" (Luke 2:4–5). Did Mary go to Bethlehem with Joseph simply because she was his wife? Or did she go also in order to register there in person, because she too belonged to the house of David? The Evangelist mentions only the first reason, but this does not exclude the second one.[5]

If we confined ourselves to these texts, the only ones we have on the subject, we should have to conclude that Mary's Davidic origin is only a probability and not a certainty. But, on the other hand, we cannot deny her descent from David simply because she was related to Elizabeth who, born of the tribe of Levi (Luke 1:5, 36), was of the priestly and not the kingly race. Before we could do this, we should first of all have to determine the exact nature of the relationship and prove that it was a natural and not simply a legal bond. And then we should have to prove further that her relationship with Elizabeth was due to descent in the direct and not merely the collateral line.

Ancient Traditions

About the year 110 A.D., St. Ignatius of Antioch spoke several times of Jesus Christ, the Son of David according to the flesh (Eph. 18:2; 20:2; Rom. 7:3, Smyrn. 1:1). Did he thereby state that Mary, Christ's Mother, truly belonged to the family of David? We do not know. Perhaps he, too, was thinking of mere legal descent and may have been quoting St. Paul, who uses the same formula (Rom. 1:3). However, about 150 A.D. St. Justin expressed himself more clearly and said plainly that Christ was descended from David through Mary. Writing to Trypho, he said that Christ was born "of a Virgin of the race of Abraham, of the tribe of Juda and of David" (*Dialog.* 43) and that He consented to be made flesh of her (*Ibid.* 4–5). About the same time, the *Protoevangelium of James,* not content with stating Mary's Davidic origin (chap. 10), names her mother Anne and her father Joachim for the first time and gives ample information about their lives (chaps. 1–8). They were very rich and lived near the Temple in Jerusalem; they showed proof of unusual holiness, but while they were advanced in years, they were still childless, a source of great sorrow to them. However, God, moved by their prayers, sent an angel to announce to them the end of their mourning and to foretell the illustrious future of their child. Immediately Anne consecrated to the Lord the child that was to be born (cf. 1 Sam. 1:11). To say the least, these details, reproduced by later apocryphal writings, testify to the author's great devotion to Mary and are a witness to the exceptionally high honor that was already being paid to the Blessed Virgin in the first Christian communities.[6]

Notes

1. Cf. P. Benoit, *L'Evangile selon saint Matthieu,* éd. du Cerf, Paris, 1961, p. 7 ff., 39 ff.
2. Cf. L. Vaganay, *Le Problème Synoptique* (Paris–Tournai, 1954), pp. 254, 260–262.
3. Cf. Deut. 25:5 ff.; Matt. 22:24; see R. de Vaux, *op. cit.,* vol. 1, p. 66 ff., 85 ff.; *Bible de Jérusalem,* ed. 1956, p. 1290, note a.

4. Cf. RB, 1911, pp. 443-451; M. J. Lagrange, *L'Evangile selon saint Luc*, 1921, p. 116 ff.; *Verbum Domini*, 1925, p. 41 ff.; 1927, p. 267 ff.

5. Some manuscripts (e.g., *Syrsin.*) specifically mention that Mary went to be enrolled as a descendant of David also.

6. Cf. Amiot, *Evangiles Apocryphes* (Paris: Fayard, 1952), p. 45 ff.; J. Hervieux, *Ce que l'Evangile ne dit pas* (Fayard, Paris, 1958), p. 22 ff.

7

Her Birth

Date

THE ANCIENT DOCUMENTS do not tell us the precise date of Mary's birth, but it does not follow that we cannot determine it to within a few years. We are able to do so by making several cross-checks; but since the details are of interest mainly to experts, we shall give only the essential points here.[1]

At the time of Christ's birth Mary must have been about fifteen years old, for the customs of the day in Israel decreed that girls should be married soon after puberty and after a period of betrothal. If we determine the date of Christ's birth, therefore, we can easily count back fifteen years and so arrive at Mary's date of birth. But is it possible to fix the date of our Lord's Nativity?

For a long time people believed that it had been done satisfactorily by a sixth century monk named Dionysius Exiguus ("the Little"), who in fact is responsible for the dating of the Christian era that we now follow. Dionysius based his work on a strict relationship between two chronological indications given by St. Luke's Gospel. He read there that Jesus was thirty years old at the start of His public life, although the text actually says *"about* thirty years of age" (Luke 3:23). He also found there that St. John the Baptist began to preach in the fifteenth year of the Emperor Tiberius (Luke 3:1-3). He was convinced that the years of Tiberius's reign should be calculated from the death of Augustus in the year 766 from the foundation of Rome. Hence the fifteenth year of Tiberius's reign would correspond with the year 782 from the foundation of Rome. Correlating these two indications from the Gospel, Dionysius concluded that Jesus was born in the year 753 from the foundation of Rome, and he fixed on this year as the beginning of the Christian era. Therefore, Mary was born about fifteen years before the beginning of our era.

But Dionysius's calculations are no longer accepted. We know that the third Gospel's chronological data about our Lord's being thirty years old and about the beginning of the fifteenth year of Tiberius can be interpreted differently. We also know from another source that Jesus was born at least five years before the date fixed by the good monk, that is, five years before the Christian era as now calculated.

The Gospel tells us that our Savior came into the world when Herod the Great was still alive and residing in Jerusalem; for it was from the capital that the king, fearing he would be dethroned by his young messianic rival, gave the order for the massacre of all male children of two years or less in the whole neighborhood of Bethlehem (Matt. 2:16).

And history tells us that Herod died at the end of March or the beginning of April, just before the Jewish Passover of the year 749 from the foundation of Rome. We know, too, that the disease from which he ultimately died, had forced him to leave Jerusalem for Jericho in the autumn of the preceding year at the latest.

Hence we know that, at the earliest, Jesus was born in the year 748 from the foundation of Rome, not in 753 as Dionysius would have it; that is, Christ was born at least five years before the Christian era as now reckoned. But, for all that, can we determine the precise date of the Nativity? There would be no difficulty if we knew more about the census of Quirinius which brought the Holy Family to the cave in Bethlehem (Luke 2:1). For the present, however, let us follow the example of many authors and put the census, and hence Christ's birth, in the year 6 or 7 before our era. Therefore Mary must have been born about 20 B.C.

The Rebuilding of the Temple

Our Lady's birth coincided with the great reconstruction of the Temple which Jerusalem witnessed some twenty years before our era. The citizens knew that Herod had mobilized thousands of workers, 11,000 to be exact, and that he intended to build a truly wondrous edifice. They were very proud of their Temple, as were the Apostles themselves later.[2]

But the city did not know that at the same time another temple was being built in silence, north of the city walls and little more than a hundred yards from the site of the marvelous building they were waiting for. A child named Mary had just been born in a place called Bethzatha, in the house of Anne and Joachim. The event made so little stir that tradition has almost nothing to say about it, and is instead embellished with legends to fill up the gaps.

A Temple Greater than Herod's

Appearances are deceptive, it is said, and in this case they were more so than ever; for history was to reveal how much greater the second of these temples was than the first.

Despite its massive foundations, its perimeter of more than 1700 yards, and its superstructure that rivaled the most beautiful in the world, Herod's Temple did not endure. It stood for only 90 years, until 70 A.D., when the armies of Titus burned it to the ground. Furthermore, it was the dwelling place of the Heavenly Father in a cosmological and symbolic sense only, as St. Stephen and St. Paul were to say: "Not in houses made by hands does the Most High dwell . . . , 'The heaven is my throne, and the earth a footstool for my feet. What house will you build me, says the Lord? . . . Did not my hand make all this?'" (Acts 7:48 f.; 14:27; Isa. 66:1 f.).

While the Temple symbolically determined the Divine Presence, it did so only locally, so that the people had to go to Jerusalem to find God (Ps. 84:126). Even then, it benefited the Jews alone, because any pagan that set foot within the sacred boundaries of the Temple incurred the death penalty.[3]

Mary, the child that had just been born, would never know the corruption of the tomb; glorified in soul, she was also glorified in body, as the dogma of the Assumption teaches. God would make Himself personally present in her, and she, as Mother of the Incarnate Word, would carry within her the Emmanuel, "God with us." While benefiting from God's presence in her, she would cause the whole of mankind to profit therefrom. Full of grace from the moment she herself was conceived, in view of her divine maternity, she would give the world her Son, in whom "dwells all the fullness of the Godhead bodily" (Col. 2:9), who allows all those who wish, to share in that fullness (John 1:12, 16; 6:56; Col. 2, 11).

Practical Lessons

We can learn many lessons from the simultaneous yet highly contrasting advent of the last two Jewish "sanctuaries." Our trust in Providence is strengthened thereby because God, to whom everything is present, foreknew the approaching devastation of the Jewish people and their Temple. Accordingly, He prepared in due time a new Temple and a new people.[4]

Furthermore, certain characteristics of God's work stand out clearly; it was interior, universal, and freely done. Herod's Temple rose only at great expenditure of materials and labor; it was not given but rather acquired. But the Temple that was Mary, was a gift that no human dignity could prepare for or merit; it came from God's goodness alone. The whole value of Herod's Temple was, in a sense, plainly visible for all men to see; the most striking thing about it was its outward appearance. But in Mary there were only interior qualities to catch the attention; what counted in her case was that which happened within. Finally, as we have seen, Herod's Temple limited the benefit of God's presence to the Jewish people; but Mary was to cause the whole universe to profit therefrom.

From this we can learn to be on our guard against our unceasing tendency to glory in our own spiritual edifice, instead of seeing it as something for which to thank God. We also find here an invitation to avoid impressions based solely on appearances, no matter what these appearances may be, and to esteem only real, basic qualities. If we do so, we shall acquire a more realistic idea of the social dimensions of our Christianity.

What does it matter, then, if we do not know all the details of Mary's ancestry and childhood, or if we must reject much of what the apocryphal gospels tell us about these matters? We know the essentials, and these are amply sufficient to guide us along the path that leads to God.

The Name Given to the Child: Mary

There is no doubt that when the predestined Mother of God was born, she received the name Mary. She is called by this name by St. Matthew (five times), St. Mark (once) and especially St. Luke (thirteen times). No doubt the name was then pronounced Mariam and not Miriam as it had been when Hebrew was widely spoken in Palestine. It was then a fairly common name, once made famous by Aaron's sister (Exod. 15:20), and, much later, well-known as the name of one of Herod the Great's unfortunate wives.[5] Many others bore it; for example, Mary Magdalene, Mary of Bethany, Mary the mother of James, and Mary the mother of John Mark.

The scientific etymology of the name remains uncertain. The popular meaning, at present the one most accepted, is "Mistress," "Princess," or "Lady." It probably came, as did Martha, from the Aramaic word *Mârâ,* meaning "Lord." Thus, by her very given name, the Blessed Virgin is "our Lady."

Ancient Traditions

According to the *Protoevangelium of James* (chap. 5), Mary was born near the Temple in Jerusalem. The canonical

Gospels say nothing about this, but merely state that the Virgin lived in Nazareth at the time of the Annunciation and thereafter (Luke 1:26; 2:4; cf. Matt. 2:23). Suffice it to say that the texts leave us perplexed. Still, according to several scholars, archeology gives us "enough assurance to venerate on the spot now dedicated to St. Anne (north of Jerusalem) the birth (place) of the Blessed Virgin" (Dressaire). In fact, this site near the Probatica Pool has a large twelfth century Romanesque church that replaced or incorporated some very ancient religious structures, the oldest of which, built over a group of rocky caverns, probably went back to Constantine the Great (280–337) and was perhaps built right over Mary's birthplace.[6]

The Feast of Our Lady's Nativity has been celebrated in the East since the middle of the sixth century but it was not introduced into the West until the following century.[7]

Notes

1. U. Holzmeister, *Chronologia Vitae Christi* (Rome, 1933), pp. 15–45.
2. On this new Temple in Jerusalem, cf. Flavius Josephus, *Jewish War*, V, 1 ff.; Mark 13:1, see also A. Parrot, *Le Temple de Jérusalem* (Paris, 1954), p. 58 ff.
3. Cf. Y. Congar, *Le Mystère du Temple* (Paris, 1958), p. 282 ff. (tr. London: Burns & Oates, 1962).
4. The only perfect Temple of the Godhead was the humanity of Christ (Col. 2:9), but from the Annunciation to the Nativity Mary was the temple of this Temple and through grace partook of the divine life of Christ's humanity (cf. Y. Congar, *op. cit.*, p. 288).
5. Cf. Flavius Josephus, *Jewish Antiquities*, XV, 7, 9 f.
6. Cf. Vincent-Abel, *Jérusalem nouvelle*, Paris, 1926, vol. 2, pp. 669–742; Dressaire, *Jérusalem à travers les siècles* (Paris, 1931), p. 436 ff.
7. Cf. D. Flicoteaux, *Mystères et fêtes de la Vierge Marie* (Paris, 1956), *La Maison-Dieu*, no. 54, p. 95 ff.; *Notre-Dame dans l'Année Liturgique*, *Maria, Etudes sur la Sainte Vierge*, vol. 1, Paris, 1949, p. 225 f. (*La Liturgie Mariale en Occident*, by Dom Capelle, pp. 217–245).

8

The Annunciation

Now in the sixth month[1] the angel Gabriel was sent by God to a town of Galilee called Nazareth, to a virgin betrothed to a man named Joseph, of the house of David, and the virgin's name was Mary. And coming to her, he said (to her): "Hail, full of grace, the Lord is with thee."[2] But she was troubled at this word and asked herself what this greeting meant. Then the angel said to her: "Do not be afraid, Mary, for thou hast found grace before God. Behold, thou shalt conceive and shalt bring forth a son, and thou shalt give him the name Jesus. He shall be great and shall be called the Son of the Most High; the Lord God will give him the throne of David his father; he shall reign forever

over the house of Jacob, and his kingdom shall have no end."
But Mary said to the angel: "How shall this be done, since
I do not know man?" The angel gave her (this) answer:
"The Holy Spirit shall come upon thee, and the power of the
Most High shall overshadow thee; that is why the child (shall
be) holy, he shall be called Son of God.[3] And behold, thy
kinswoman, Elizabeth, has herself conceived a son in her
old age, and this is the sixth month for her who was called
barren, for nothing is impossible to God." Then Mary
said: "Behold the handmaid of the Lord; be it done to me
according to thy word." And the angel departed from her.

The Humble Virgin

At the time of the Annunciation, and for reasons unknown to us, Mary was living in the village of Nazareth,
which lay some eighty-seven miles north of Jerusalem and was
called a town only in the juridical sense of the term.[4] Mary
was a virgin but was already betrothed to Joseph, a young
carpenter in the locality, one of the numerous descendants
of the ancient family of David. Hence she must have then
been at the age when Jewish maidens were betrothed, that
is, fourteen years old at the most.[5] She would not be installed
in her fiancé's house as his bride for several months yet,
that is, until after her return from the Visitation (Luke
1:56; Matt. 1:18 ff.). Although the Annunciation would
take effect immediately, it would not entail any embarrass-
ment for Mary because, according to the Jewish Law, the
honor of an intended bride was already protected by her
fiancé's name.[6]

What were the events of Mary's life before this time?
The apocryphal legends, full of a Marian devotion that is
quite ingenuous, speak of her Presentation and edifying life
in the Temple from the age of three until puberty.[7] The scene

is modeled on the presentation of the young Samuel (1 Sam. 1:24 ff.), but "its fullest significance does not overstate Mary's purity and consecration to her God" (J. J. Weber). The Gospel tells us nothing about this period in our Lady's life and speaks of her for the first time only in relationship to the Messias-Savior. The Annunciation was the coming of this Messias; it crowned the announcement of the Precursor's birth made six months before (Luke 1:11 ff., 26), and fulfilled all the prophesies of the Old Testament.[8] Viewed from this angle, it has an ineffable grandeur, a grandeur which was to be infinitely increased by the gradual realization that the newly-conceived Messias was divine. It was the sublime counter-stroke to the fall of our first parents and opened a whole new era. The Incarnation that followed upon Mary's acceptance was to blot out the disastrous consequences of Adam's refusal to obey in the Garden of Eden. Humanity was transfigured by the new Eve and regained the divine life of grace.

In their paintings, artists have tried to portray the invisible grandeur of the scene by endowing the humble Virgin of Nazareth with the appearance and dress of a queen, and turning her poor dwelling into a veritable palace. But we can readily pardon their unfaithfulness to reality, while we ourselves keep more strictly to the facts of history.

Nowadays we think of the Virgin of the Annunciation as she really was, living in her village of a few hundred souls, far from the capital and in the heart of a region inhabited by pagans. We know that her home was half mud-cabin, half limestone cave, set into the side of a hill. We accept the fact that she was busy with the chores of a rather primitive household: going about barefooted, carrying her pitcher to the only available fountain about 650 yards away, sitting on the ground, turning the hand-mill to grind the grain, baking the bread, weaving and sewing the rough garments. In short, she did the same things as all the other girls of her age.[9]

Far from being scandalized by this picture of Mary's earthly life at the time of the Annunciation, we find it an incentive to shed many of our illusions about the greatness of this world. All the Blessed Virgin's glory lay beyond her apparent abasement and within her pure, loving, selfsacrificing heart. She was full of divine grace, as the angel would tell her later (Luke 1:28), and for this reason was more worthy than all others to become the Mother of the Son of God.[10] It has been truly said that God's choice of this outward appearance and setting for such an exalted mission shows His intention to stress most emphatically the gratuitous, interior, and universal nature of that mission.[11]

The Divine Message

For Gabriel, the angel making the Annunciation, it was the third messianic mission. At the time of the Machabean insurrection, he had had the task of explaining the secret of the last days (Dan. 8:15 ff.; 9:21 ff.), and very recently, scarcely six months before his present mission, he had predicted the imminent conception of the Precursor, John (Luke 1:5 ff.). This time, however, he was to make known the birth of the Messias himself. In truth, he was the angel of the good tidings of salvation.

When Gabriel appeared suddenly in our Lady's room (Luke 1:28), she did not yet know anything about the recent conception of the Precursor (Luke 1:36). His greeting to her, "Hail!" expressed, in Aramaic, a wish for peace (shalom), in Greek, a wish for joy (chaïré). This was followed by an extraordinary title, used as a proper name: "Hail, full of grace!" and by a formula that gave it a moral and supernatural meaning: "The Lord (is) with thee." In biblical language, the Lord God is with those whom He favors with His active presence. Mary was the object of this presence and of the divine benevolence,[12] and permanently so because the verb used was in the form of the perfect (*kecharitoméne*). Hence she was so much God's *favored one* that this title could replace her own name. In his Bull *Ineffabilis* (Dec. 8, 1854), Pope Pius IX was to draw from this text an argument in favor of the Immaculate Conception. Modern exegetes, following the Greek Fathers, believe that the angel's greeting was not simply an ordinary salutation but rather an invitation to the messianic joy spoken of by the prophets, especially by Sophonias, who said to the town of Sion, a prefigurement of Mary; "Be glad and exult with all your heart, O daughter Jerusalem. . . . The King of Israel, the Lord, is in your midst. . . . Fear not . . . , the Lord, your God, is in your midst, a mighty savior" (3:14–17). In any case, it is not very probable that Mary immediately recognized the scriptural parallel.[13] However, the great perturbation that the angel's greeting aroused in her shows that she suspected that it had a higher meaning, which she tried to unravel (Luke 1:29).

Having caught her attention with his first words, Gabriel told her not to be afraid at what he had said. Zachary, who had trembled at the mere sight of the angel, had received the same consolation (Luke 1:13). The whole history of Israel had taught both our Lady and Zachary how formidable the divine interventions could be.[14] But this time, the angel assured Mary, the intervention was benevolent, because she had "found grace before God" (Luke 1:30), the scriptural way of saying that she was exceptionally pleasing to Him and that she was worthy of new favors (cf. Gen. 6:8; Exod. 33:12; Judges 6:17; Esther 7:3). Thus she was prepared for the announcement of a joyous message.

In fact, the angel informed her that she was to become the mother of the Messias. He told her in a way well suited to the Jewish mentality of the day, in terms that were inspired in form and substance by the best known prophecies of royal messianism in the Old Testament. Mary was to bring forth a son named Jesus (Luke 1:31; cf. Isa. 14), an exceptional child, so blessed by God that he would be called the Son of the Most High and would be the heir of David his father and the eternal leader of the Chosen People (Luke 1:32 f.; cf. 2 Sam. 7:12 ff.; Isa. 9:5 f.; Dan. 7:14, 27).[15] However, for the moment there was nothing that went beyond the idea of royal messianism.

The Explanatory Dialogue

No Jewish woman in that age of feverish expectation of the Messias (cf. Luke 3:15) could have heard the angel's announcement without being overjoyed, and Mary was certainly no exception. Had not the angel himself invited her to rejoice? Yet before she gave way completely to joy, she wished to ascertain how she should act in order to fulfill her divine mission: "How shall this happen, since I do not know man?" (Luke 1:34). Asked by a betrothed girl, this question would normally refer to the future and would indicate that conjugal relations had not been contemplated. Furthermore, it shows that "Mary reasoned along the lines of her contemporaries who looked for the Messias to be born according to the ordinary laws of nature."[16] The vast majority of Catholic authors see here the proof that Mary had resolved to remain forever a virgin, as we shall see later on. She had, as it were, the impression of being between two indications of God's will that were hard to reconcile—one had inspired her to remain a virgin, while the second now asked her to become a mother. The question she addressed to the angel therefore meant that she was looking to God to show her the way she must act. There was nothing reprehensible in her question, because far from being reprimanded as Zachary had been (Luke 1:19 f.), she would soon be praised for having believed (Luke 1:45).

The angel immediately answered her question, but did so in scriptural language adorned on this occasion with parallelism. He revealed the mysterious element in the messianic motherhood (Luke 1:35); Mary would remain a virgin but would still become a mother through a unique miracle. The Holy Spirit would come upon her, as He had come upon the waters at the creation of the world (Gen. 1:2), and once more He would be a creative and vivifying divine force. The power of the Most High would overshadow her, as before the cloud, symbol of God's presence, had covered the sanctuary of Israel and filled the Ark of the Covenant with the glory of Yahweh (Exod. 40:35). In this context and as a reply to Mary's question, this was tantamount at least to saying that Jesus, as man, would have no father but God, and that His conception would come solely from the power of God and His Spirit.

Having made this revelation, the angel added: "*That is why* the child (shall be) holy, he shall be called the Son of God" (Luke 1:35*). Was he thus asserting, as many scholars believe, that the child would be the Son of God in the strict sense? And did he regard this as a direct consequence of God's intervention? If he did, the divine intervention would mean that Mary's womb would become the Tabernacle of God himself and that He would become present there.[17] "The mere affirmation of Mary's virginal conception would not be a sufficient reason for Jesus' holiness, let alone His divine sonship, unless we take this sonship in a purely metaphorical sense, as does Maldonatus" (A. Feuillet).

Mary's Acceptance

Did Mary realize immediately and clearly that the Messias who was to be born of her would also be God? As we shall see, the authors are not agreed on this point. At all events, she had just learned that God had the power to reconcile her promised maternity with her virginity by means of an extraordinary intervention. The angel next went on to ask her to believe in and consent to this intervention by revealing to her the unexpected and already well-established pregnancy of her aged kinswoman Elizabeth. This miracle, he added, clearly proved that "nothing is impossible to God" (Luke 1:37*; Gen. 18:14), and that for Him the laws of nature are not insurmountable obstacles.

The narrative demonstrates how much God takes into account the free will of His creatures. He treated Mary as a person, as a free agent giving her consent with full knowledge of the circumstances. The act of faith He requested and the consent He awaited were not long in coming. The angel had scarcely finished answering Mary's question when she replied: "Behold the handmaid of the Lord; be it done to me according to thy word" (Luke 1:38). Then the angel withdrew, his mission accomplished. In assuming the biblical title "handmaid of the Lord," Mary expressed her total, holy submission to God's will and showed that she was completely at His disposal for His divine plan of messianic salvation. To an Israelite, a servant of God (*ebed Yahweh*) meant an adorer of God, one who bent his own will to whatever God willed and rendered Him the most perfect homage possible. In the Greek vernacular, the word "servant" ordinarily meant "slave" in the legal sense, that is, one who did not have his freedom.[18]

Mary's acceptance was the antithesis of Eve's refusal, and it immediately took effect by being the starting point of Redemption, just as the first woman's refusal had been at the origin of the fall of mankind.

Ancient Traditions

Since 1954 the Franciscan Custody of the Holy Land has been working to restore and preserve the ruins of the ancient church built over the Grotto of the Annunciation in Nazareth. The work done after the demolition of the church (1730–1877) has had important results. The medieval church, brought to light by the excavations of 1907–1909, is now better known. The Byzantine church, the floor of which served as the base for the medieval structure, has been more thoroughly explored and the date of its erection put back to about 427 A.D. Christian inscriptions found on remains there prove that a small single-naved chapel preceded the Byzantine building. This chapel, built in the third century by Count Joseph of Tiberias and destroyed in the first part of the fifth century, shows that this spot has been venerated almost since Gospel times. The rocky cavity that extends to the north of the sacred site contains a whole network of caves, olive-presses, cisterns and silos, which are linked by ventilation ducts and were formerly the basements of ancient dwellings that have now disappeared. The inhabitants were farmers, and pieces of pottery found there date from the Herodian period, that is, from Mary's own day.[19] The popular legend gives 1291 as the year in which Mary's "Holy House" was miraculously transported to Loreto.

About 650 yards north of the Grotto of the Annunciation, in the direction of Tiberias, stands the Greek Orthodox church of St. Gabriel. Beneath this structure, which is the successor to some very ancient edifices, rises the only spring in Nazareth, which feeds the Fountain of the Virgin nearby. According to the *Protoevangelium of James* (10:1–3), it was here, at either the spring or the fountain, that the angel first greeted the Blessed Virgin, frightening her and causing her to flee to her home, so that he had to follow her there to deliver his message. The apocryphal writer, unlike the Evangelist, does not emphasize the messianic implications of the event, but rather seems to be preoccupied with establishing the virginal conception of the Child to come or, to put it another way, the physical inviolability of the Mother: hence the feeling of panic which he attributed to her.

Constantinople, Syria, Palestine, and Egypt celebrated the liturgical Feast of the Annunciation at an early date, certainly at the beginning of the fifth century or even perhaps at the end of the fourth, and the same holds good for Ravenna in Italy. No mention is made of it at Rome until the pontificate of Gregory the Great (590–604), and it was celebrated there on the Wednesday of Ember Week in December, not on March 25. There is no evidence that the latter date, which is a corollary of Christmas Day, was used before the close of the fifth century.[20]

Notes

1. That is, the sixth month after Elizabeth had conceived the Precursor, John the Baptist (Luke 1:24,36).
2. Some manuscripts add here: "Blessed art thou among women," no doubt a borrowing from the account of the Visitation (Luke 1:42).
3. The Vulgate Latin has: "Therefore the Holy (One) to be born of thee shall be called the Son of God."
4. Cf. W. Corswant, *Dictionnaire d'Archéologie Biblique* (Paris, 1956), p. 312.

5. Cf. R. de Vaux, *op. cit.*, vol. 1, p. 57. *The Protoevangelium of James* gives Mary's age as sixteen at the time of Christ's birth.

6. Cf. R. de Vaux, *ibid.*

7. Cf. *Protoevangelium of James*, chaps. 7–8; see also J. Hervieux, *op. cit.*, p. 105 ff.

8. Cf. R. Laurentin, *op. cit.*, p. 105 ff.

9. Cf. *Les Cahiers de la Vierge*, no. 3, *Notre-Dame à Nazareth* (Paris, 1934), p. 31 ff.

10. Cf. *ibid.*, p. 52 ff.

11. Cf. J. Galot, *Mary in the Gospel* (tr. by Sr. Maria Constance, S.C.H.) (Westminster: Newman, 1964), p. 6 ff.

12. Cf. *Maria, Etudes sur la Sainte Vierge*, vol. 6, p. 33.

13. Cf. *ibid.*, p. 31.

14. Cf. M. E. Boismard, *Le Prologue de Saint Jean* (Paris, 1953), p. 88 f.

15. Cf. DBS, article on "Messianisme," pp. 1174–1190, by A. Gelin.

16. J. J. Weber, *op. cit.*, p. 28, note 6.

17. Cf. *Maria*, vol. 6, p. 34; RB, 1958, p. 428; R. Laurentin, *op. cit.*, p. 78; S. Lyonnet, *Le récit de l'Annonciation et la maternité divine de la Sainte Vierge*, in *L'Ami du Clergé*, 1956, p. 43–46.

18. Cf. J. Huby, *Saint Paul, épître aux Romains*, 1957, p. 36 f.

19. Cf. RB, 1956, p. 80 ff.; 1960, p. 386 f.; 1962, pp. 418–420: *La Vie Intellectuelle*, 1955, p. 23 ff. We know that relatives of Jesus were still to be found there as late as the third century (Eusebius, *Historia ecclesiastica* I, vii, 2).

20. Cf. *La Vie Spirituelle*, Dec., 1926, p. 296 ff.

9

Mary's Virginal Resolve

The Problem: First Answers

Wᴇ ᴀʀᴇ ɴᴏᴛ ᴄᴏɴᴄᴇʀɴᴇᴅ here with Mary's *state* of virginity before the conception and birth of her Son (*virginitas ante partum*), a teaching that, since apostolic times, has never been denied by Catholics.[1] We are dealing merely with the *motive* for her virginity. Was hers simply the normal virginity of a girl waiting to be married, or was it due to a deliberate resolve resulting from the influence of grace and the attraction of virginity?[2]

The first Christian centuries say nothing about the matter; it was not even mentioned until the time of Origen (185–254) and then only very tentatively. But starting with St. Augustine (354–430), the common teaching was that

Mary had made a resolve or even a vow of virginity well before the Annunciation. This is what the holy Bishop of Hippo wrote on the subject:

> What made Mary's virginity . . . so pleasing to God was not the fact that it had been preserved by the conception of Christ, which prevented her husband from despoiling her of it, but rather that, even before she had conceived, she had already vowed it to God. . . . This is clearly evident from the answer she gave the angel when he announced her maternity to her: "How shall this be done, since I do not know man?" These words certainly would not have been said if she had not already made a vow to the Lord to remain a virgin. But since Jewish custom was then opposed to this, she was betrothed to a just man, who, far from taking from her that which she had vowed to God, was to be the faithful guardian thereof (*De sancta virginitate*, IV).

Recent Opinions

Because it is certainly an anachronism to speak in this context of a vow of virginity properly so called, as St. Augustine does, modern authors prefer to call it a decision (S. Lyonnet) or even simply a desire (P. Synave) which Mary did not formulate more precisely until she became betrothed to Joseph and received his consent (Cardinal Cajetan).

From the beginning of the Reformation (1517–1546), Protestant exegetes, with some rare exceptions, did not hold that Mary had contemplated such a resolution. Some Catholic authors in our day share this point of view, but they base their opinion on interpretations of the Annunciation narrative which do not sufficiently respect its unity, the normal meaning of the words used in it, Mary's ability to understand what the angel said, or his ability to express himself clearly. These authors believe that they find confirmation of their opinion in what they call the absence of a religious climate favorable to the idea of virginity or voluntary celibacy in the era in which Mary lived.

We shall review briefly some of the Catholic theories opposed to the idea of Mary's having made a resolve to remain a virgin. According to one of the oldest of these theories, Mary understood that the angel was announcing to her a conception that had already taken place, hence her question: "How can this be since I am still a virgin?" This is scarcely in accord with the rest of the text (Luke 1:35 ff.; 1:45), and even less with the solemnity of the whole narrative. It presumes that the Evangelist completely misunderstood the incident, that the angel used astonishingly inexact language at the most critical moment, although at first he had been careful to catch Mary's attention (Luke 1:28–30); and it disregards the parallel announcement to Zachary where all the evidence requires the future of the verb, which would demand that we read here "Behold, you *shall* conceive!" and not "Behold, you have conceived!"[3]

According to another theory, the angel announced to Mary that she was to conceive immediately, and Mary, whose marriage was not to take place for several months yet, answered quite simply that such a conception was impossible because she was still only engaged. The proponents of this theory make the mistake of applying modern ideas about engagement and marriage to the completely different world in which Mary lived. Furthermore they attribute to the angel a precision of expression that he did not use, for he said nothing about the date or moment of the conception.

A more recent theory is based upon the meaning of the conjunction Mary used in her reply to the angel. The advocates of this theory say that her reply should be translated "How shall this be done *because then* (*e'pei*) I would have to remain a virgin?" She was surprised at the role the angel was offering her, because she knew from the prophecy of Isaias (7:14) that the mother of the Messias would be a virgin; and she was objecting to the angel's announcement, not because she had resolved to remain a virgin, but rather because she intended to get married and had already given her word by becoming betrothed. She could not see how she could reconcile her betrothal and intention to get married with the honor of becoming the virgin mother of the Messias, which the angel was offering her. But this theory is based merely on an interpretation of the conjunction that lacks support in the present instance; it assumes gratuitously that Mary was referring to the Messianic text of Isaias (7:14). The proponents of the theory forget that, in common with all her contemporaries, Mary most probably did not interpret Isaias' prophecy in the strict sense of a virginal conception. Furthermore, such a meaning would not at all fit in with the immediate context of the narrative (Luke 1:35 ff.).[4]

The immense majority of Catholic authors are convinced that only a resolve of virginity on Mary's part can make the Annunciation narrative plausible, which is the position we took in the preceding chapter. These authors are also convinced that the religious climate in Mary's day was not as impervious as some believe to the idea of virginity or voluntary celibacy. Let's examine this last point a little more closely.

Biblical Beginnings of Voluntary Virginity

Those who deny that Mary resolved to remain a virgin, hold that such a resolution would have run counter to biblical teaching and practices. The entire Old Testament, they say, was marked by an emphasis on marriage and fecundity; God's blessing then consisted in having many worldly goods and hence many children who would ensure that those goods would be productive and would remain in the family. Conversely, God's curse consisted in poverty, sterility, and lack of offspring. Supporters of this opinion add that in view of the messianic future of her people, every Jewish girl must have wanted to become a mother so as to be able, perhaps, to assist in the coming of the Messias. Hence Mary's resolve would have been a clean break with the past, a complete innovation, an exceptional case resulting from a miracle of grace.[5]

This is assuredly the impression we get from reading the more ancient books of the Bible.[6] But when we examine the more recent books, those dating from the last two centuries before our era, we see that the outlook had changed. In fact, these books finally revealed clearly the resurrection of the dead, the immortality of the soul, and the idea of a spiritual reward in the next life.[7] Thus they allowed those who wished to do so, to fix their minds and hearts on aims other than the passing prosperity of this world and that completely relative mode of survival after death which consisted in living on in one's posterity. Furthermore, they praised chaste widowhood, condemned the evil inclinations of the flesh, and placed virtuous sterility above sinful fecundity.[8] And in the light of these later Old Testament books, we see that the more ancient ones spoke about marriage and fecundity for the whole race rather than for each individual of that race, that they were stressing, for the moment, only one aspect of a complex question, and were making necessary concessions to prevailing customs.[9]

Voluntary Celibacy in Mary's Day

Those who deny Mary's virginal resolve believe also that such a resolution would not have been in accordance with contemporary Jewish practice. They say that the Jews did not tolerate celibacy among them and that they were obsessed by the fear of sterility.

In reality, however, marriage did not become obligatory among the Jews until much later.[10] In Mary's day, and even in the years preceding her birth, voluntary celibacy was practised in Israel both by men and women, as attested by several trustworthy witnesses. Pliny the Elder (died 79 A.D.) in his *Natural History* (V, 17) speaks about the Essenes, who lived lives of celibacy and poverty among the palm trees on the shores of the Dead Sea. Flavius Josephus (37–94 A.D.) distinguishes between two categories of Essenes, those who married and those who chose to live in celibacy. The latter, he says, "disdain marriage for themselves but adopt the children of others . . . and treat them as if they were their own."[11] Philo of Alexandria (died 50 A.D.) states specifically that the Essenes scorned marriage by practising complete and permanent continence so as not to break the bond that existed between them; and he also mentions the existence of the Therapeutae, a sect founded in Egypt many years before, and composed of men and women who chose to practise perfect chastity.[12]

Documents recently discovered in the caves at Qumrân, north-east of the Dead Sea, seem to confirm this testimony to the practice of voluntary celibacy by a section of the Essene community. Thus the *Manual of Discipline* or *Rule* of the community, which deals with men only, shows that they lived in such close association with each other that the least degree of family life would have been impossible for them.[13]

Conclusion

Therefore those who say that Mary would not have dreamed of making a resolve to remain a virgin reject the most obvious meaning of the Gospel narrative of the Annunciation in favor of some labored explanation of the text. They fail to take sufficiently into account the biblical beginnings that slowly led souls to higher concepts of fecundity. And they do not pay due attention to those Jewish communities that, at the dawn of our era, chose a life of voluntary celibacy, thus creating a climate favorable to later imitators.[14]

Notes

1. Cf. Jouassard, *Marie à Travers la Patristique; Maria, Etudes sur la Vierge* (Paris, 1949), vol. 1, pp. 69–157.

2. Cf. *Masses Ouvrières*, May, 1958, pp. 15–32, J. Cantinat, *Le propos de virginité de Marie et le célibat des Esséniens*; J. Galot, *Mary in the gospel* (Westminster: Newman, 1964). pp. 25–47.

3. *Masses Ouvrières, ibid.*, p. 18 f.; J. Galot, *op. cit.*, p. 31 ff.

4. Cf. RB, 1956, pp. 346–374, *L'Annonce à Marie*, J. P. Audet.

5. Cf. *La chasteté et la religieuse d'aujourd'hui*, Paris, éd. du Cerf, chap. 1.

6. Cf. DBS, article on "Mariage"; *Vocabulaire de Théologie Biblique* (Paris, 1962), p. 577 ff.; A. Gelin, *La Famille dans l'histoire du peuple de Dieu, Cahiers Marials*, Jan.-Feb., 1959, pp. 3–10.

7. Cf. Dan. 12:2; 2 Mach. 6:26; 7:23; Wisd. 3–5; see also R. Martin-Achart, *De la Mort à la Résurrection d'après l'Ancien Testament* (Paris, 1956). (Author is a Protestant.)

8. Cf. Judith 16:24; Ecclus. 23:4 ff.; 26:9 f.; Wisd. 3:13; 4:1 ff.; Tob. 6:18.

9. Cf. *Masses Ouvrières, loc. cit.*, pp. 21–25; E. Gilson, *Saint Thomas d'Aquin*, 1930, p. 338 ff.

10. Cf. DBS, article on "Mariage," p. 924.

11. *Jewish War*, VIII, 2.

12. Cf. Eusebius, *Praep. Ev.* VIII, 11; *Hist. Eccles.*, II, 17, 3 ff.

13. Cf. G. Vermès, *Les manuscrits du Désert de Juda*, Paris, 1953; J. T. Milik, *Dix ans de Découverte dans le Désert de Juda*, Paris, 1957.

14. J. Hervieux, *op. cit.*, pp. 32–41.

Her Faith

Before the Annunciation

W<small>E HAVE ALREADY SEEN</small> what the principal Jewish beliefs were in Mary's day,[1] and we know that she must have held them with all her heart; how else could she have found grace with God (Luke 1:30)? Even more, if she had not shared these beliefs, could she have understood when the angel came from the God of Israel to speak to her about the birth of the Messias? Her virginal resolve also reveals, in another way, the faith that inspired her. Completely inexplicable in a pagan atmosphrere, her resolution was understandable in Israel itself only in the light of the more recent revelations (about the rewards of a future life) and a fervent belief in these revelations. We can even ask if her renouncing the joys of motherhood may not have been inspired by her desire to hasten the coming of the Messias,[2] for the scribes, following the prophets, readily made this event dependent upon observances of all kinds.[3]

The apocryphal writings about Mary give us a most extravagant account of her faith when she was still very young. According to them, everything about her was miraculous: from the time of her birth until the age of three she was so solicitous about avoiding whatever was profane or impure that she would never touch the ground with her feet. From the age of three until puberty, she lived in the Temple, leading the life of a cloistered religious, or rather, of a saint on a pedestal, eating heavenly food and waited upon by angels. There is here a trace of Docetism, the heresy that reduced Christ's humanity to a mere appearance.

Faith in the Annunciation

The Annunciation, far from removing Mary from our common lot as human beings, shows her exercising faith to the full. The Holy Spirit Himself testified to her faith when He put on Elizabeth's lips her praise of the Blessed Virgin: "Blessed is she who has believed in the fulfillment of that which was said to her on the Lord's behalf" (Luke 1:45*).[4] The inspired origin of these words naturally guarantees their absolute truth. Consequently, although it has been suggested,[5] it matters little whether or not Elizabeth, comparing Mary's greeting with Zachary's muteness, concluded that our Lady had believed since she could still speak, whereas Zachary's lack of faith had been evident from his inability to speak after a similar visit from an angel. It matters just as little that, in an age now far in the past, some Fathers of the Church detected unbelief in Mary's question as to how she could become a mother.[6] With the Holy Spirit, we assert the reality of her faith and even see in it the source of her merit and blessedness, for the text states that "Blessed is she who has believed" (Luke 1:45). Our Lord confirmed this when, in reproving a woman who was crying aloud Mary's praises, He declared in so many words that Mary was more closely united to Him by her faith than by her motherhood (Luke 11:28).

God, who usually teaches slowly and patiently (Rom. 3:26; Ps. 103:8; Luke 9:55), did not proceed in easy stages in the matter of our Lady's faith. Instead, only twice did He bring her face to face with the full mystery of the motherhood which was offered to her, and in doing so He provided her with two opportunities to gain merit by believing Him solely on His word. First He announced her approaching motherhood, apparently without taking into consideration the obstacle of her resolve to remain a virgin, and without mentioning at the same time the intervention of the Holy Ghost who would reconcile the two contrary conditions, motherhood and virginity (cf. Luke 1:37). Thus He confronted her with an announcement that was basically obscure, and wished her to believe firmly in it. The question she then asked (Luke 1:34) implied belief, not doubt as in Zachary's case, since, far from being reprimanded as he had been (cf. Luke 1:18–20), she was praised (Luke 1:45). Only afterward did God tell her that He would intervene directly to reconcile her virginity and her maternity, a concept that demanded a second act of faith in His word, an act that she made by giving her consent: "Behold the handmaid of the Lord; be it done to me according to thy word" (Luke 1:38). The Gospel goes on to show that God, while requiring this second act of faith, which was even more extraordinary than the first, also willed to make it easy for her. In fact, after explaining how the birth would be accomplished, the angel gave Mary a sign, a tangible proof of the divine omnipotence which she could verify, namely, the unexpected pregnancy of

Elizabeth, her aged kinswoman. Then by way of inviting her to believe that God's power would come into play in her case too, he added: "For nothing is impossible to God." His words were a repetition of those of Genesis (18:14) addressed to the aged Abraham, who had just been told that he would have a son. It seems therefore that the Gospel, by quoting these same words, wished us to liken Mary's faith to that of Israel's first ancestor. Both Mary and Abraham had been faced with a paradoxical promise, and both had believed against all human hope (cf. Rom. 4:18).

Recently, a Catholic commentator on Sacred Scripture proposed a theory that would reduce our Lady's faith at the time of the Annunciation. According to him, when she replied to the angel, she was not asking about the way in which her maternity would be achieved; she was rather objecting to an impossibility, and was thereby in effect asking for a sign to prove that the angel's prophecy could come true. And in fact the angel did confirm what he had said by giving Elizabeth's pregnancy as a sign, which she set out to verify the moment he left. Examples from the Old Testament, this author continues, prove that there was nothing reprehensible about asking for a sign (Exod. 3:10 ff.; Judges 6:15 ff.; 1 Sam. 10:1 ff.; Jer. 1:5 ff.). Zachary himself asked for one (Luke 1:18) and was given it by being struck dumb (Luke 1:20).[7] The disadvantage of this theory is that it does not respect the connection between Mary's question and the angel's answer: it makes the essential part of the answer (the manner in which Mary would conceive) secondary to the sign given (Elizabeth's pregnancy). In addition, it apparently fails to give due importance to our Lady's consent. Finally, it gratuitously treats as a kind of afterthought, and thereby weakens, what the Gospel says about the punitive nature of Zachary's being struck dumb (Luke 1:20).

Faith in Her Son's Divinity

According to Maldonatus, the angel Gabriel did not speak about the divinity of the Messias even for a moment during the Annunciation. He was concerned only with the Messias's coming and the way in which he was to be born, not with his nature.[8] Hence belief in the divinity of her son was not asked of Mary until later. This theory still has its supporters,[9] but the generality of Catholic authors, and even quite a large number of Protestant writers, hold that the second part of the angel's message does in reality announce the strictly divine sonship of the promised Messias. These authors differ only as to whether or not Mary immediately and clearly perceived the divinity of the child that she was to conceive.

Those who say that she did are impressed by the way in which God, throughout the Annunciation, treated Mary as a person, inviting her to consent only with the knowledge of the facts. This manner of acting, they say, demanded that God enlighten her on the precise nature of the proposal to which she was to consent, because there is an infinite difference between divine and human maternity.[10] They also believe that:

Just as human maternity demands a voluntary choice in order to be formally brought about . . . , so, too, Mary's divine maternity, in order to be formally such, demanded (her) free consent in her *fiat* of faith. In fact, only faith can attain to the mystery of the Word, of the Word made flesh, and only faith can freely accept this mystery. . . . Without this act of faith, (Mary) could have been only materially, or biologically, the Mother of God. . . . That is why (to state) that at the Annunciation Mary did not believe in the divinity of the Son of the Most High but only in His messianic character as God's envoy, (is to) assert that she is only materially the Mother of God.[11]

Those who are more reserved on the matter hold that the divine sonship of the Messias is contained only indirectly in the angel's words, and that a long process of Scriptural exposition is needed to discover it. Therefore, they say, we can at least deduce that God did not wish to reveal the divinity of her son to Mary at that moment and with full clarity. These authors remark further on the incomprehension which our Lady showed when, at the finding in the Temple, Jesus particularly emphasized His transcendence: "How is it that you sought me? Did you not know that I must be about my Father's business?" (Or ". . . in my Father's house?" Luke 2:50*).[12] Perhaps to this incomprehension we can add Mary's wonder at Simeon's prophecies about her Son's future (Luke 2:33) and her meditative reflection upon the events following the Nativity in Bethlehem and the finding in the Temple (Luke 2:19: ". . . pondering them in her heart"; 2:51: "And his mother kept all these things carefully in her heart"). To these authors all of this seems to indicate that our Lady's faith in her son's divinity developed gradually, in the course of her close daily contact with Him and as a result of the manifestations that followed His baptism in the Jordan. Progressive revelation is one of the characteristics of God's teaching methods. He unveils only gradually the truths He proposes, taking into account the psychological constitution of each individual and the slow development of a people's viewpoint.[13]

Her Son's Mission of Redemption

At all events, we must point out that in his message to the Blessed Virgin the angel Gabriel said nothing about the way in which her son's mission of redemption would be accomplished. He simply announced that her son would be the Messias in the traditional context of royal messianism. Of course, Mary could deduce therefrom that Jesus, the Son of David, would be His people's long-desired king; but she could not have concluded that His royalty would be essentially different from that of earthly kings, or that His sovereignty would be established by suffering and death, or that His power would extend to the whole universe. On these points Mary's faith was to develop as the events unfolded. At the beginning her faith was that of a Jew; but slowly it became a Christian faith, reaching its culmination at Pentecost, with the descent of the Holy Spirit (Acts 1:14; 2:1 ff.).

It was at Bethlehem and Jerusalem that our Lady received her first insights into her son's destiny as the *suffering* Messias: at Bethlehem, when Herod the Great menaced the life of the new-born child; at Jerusalem, when the aged Simeon predicted the unrelenting opposition to Jesus that would follow, and the suffering it would cause her, His Mother. She also tasted the sacrifices that awaited her in the future, when for three long days she lost the boy Jesus. She felt anguish then; but it was during the Passion, on Calvary especially, that she grasped fully the painful meaning of the drama of messianic redemption.

Previously, the name Jesus, which means Savior, had lost much of its impact for her because it was in common use. The angel had indeed made the symbolism of the name quite plain to Joseph: "Thou shalt call his name Jesus; for he shall save his people from their sins" (Matt. 1:21). But there were so many ways of saving a people from their sins! Could He not do it through preaching, prayer and example (cf. Isa. 42:1 ff.; 49:1 ff.)? The prophets had certainly spoken about the sufferings of the Servant of God, who was to take upon Himself the peoples' sins (Isa. 53; Ps. 22); but who in Israel saw this Servant as the Messias?[14]

Conclusions

These considerations on Mary's faith bring her very close to us and show that her destiny was not separate from ours. Like us she was asked to accept salvation as God's gift; and her manner of receiving it teaches us to be ready to answer the calls of grace and to remain resolute in our journey toward God, no matter what happens. She has become our teacher in faith. We can draw an analogy between our Lady's faith and that of the Church in general. Mary was entrusted with a mystery, and her mission was to sound its depths; the Church, in its turn, has the duty of plumbing the depths of the Christian mystery.[15] St. Thérèse of the Infant Jesus, on the very day of her death, confided to her superior: "How I would have loved to have been a priest so that I could have preached on the Virgin Mary! It seems to me that one single opportunity would have been enough for me to make people understand my thoughts about her . . . If a sermon on the Blessed Virgin is to bear fruit, it must show her life as it really was, as we catch a glimpse of it in the Gospel. . . . We have to say that she lived by faith, just as we do."[16]

Notes

1. See chapter 3 above.
2. Cf. S. Lyonnet, *loc. cit.*, p. 43.
3. Cf. *Assomption de Moïse*, I, 18; see DBS, article on "Judaïsme," p. 1236.
4. The Vulgate Latin translates Luke 1:45 as: "And blessed art thou who has believed, because those things that were said to thee by the Lord shall be accomplished." According to this version, Mary was blessed, not because of her faith, but because her expectation would not be in vain. But even in this translation, Elizabeth still bears witness to our Lady's faith at the Annunciation.
5. J. Galot, *op. cit.*, p. 51.
6. Cf. *Maria*, vol. 1, p. 78 f., 94; *Lumière et Vie*, no. 16, July 1954.

7. This is the theory advanced by F. Neirynck in *L'Evangile de Noël,* in a series called *Etudes Religieuses,* no. 749, Brussels-Paris, 1961, p. 35 ff.

8. J. Maldonatus, *Comment. sur les Quatre Evangiles,* Lyons, 1582, p. 880.

9. For example, F. Neirynck, *op. cit.,* p. 36; cf. RB, 1962, p. 193 f.

10. Cf. R. Laurentin, *op. cit.,* pp. 165–175.

11. M. D. Philippe, *Le Mystère de la Maternité divine de Marie,* in *Maria,* vol. 6, p. 379.

12. The supporters of the first theory do not think that this text presents any difficulty. They say that what Mary did not understand was not Christ's divinity but rather His showing Himself as the Messias. Cf. L. Richard, *Dieu est Amour,* Le Puy-Lyon, 1962, p. 47 f.

13. Cf. J. Galot, *op. cit.,* p. 53 ff.; K. Rahner, *Le principe fondamental de la théologie mariale,* p. 492; *Maria,* vol. 6, p. 350.

14. Cf. DBS, article on "Judaïsme," p. 1242 ff.

15. Cf. *Lumière et Vie,* no. 16, *Sainte Marie, Mère de Dieu,* p. 31 f.

16. Quoted by A. Gelin in *La Vie Spirituelle,* Aug.-Sept., 1954, p. 116.

11

Her Divine Motherhood

The Problem

Holy scripture never says explicitly that Mary was the Mother of God; it does not mention the divine maternity as such. But it does contain the idea, the meaning, behind these expressions. On the one hand Scripture reveals that Jesus was not merely man but true God, the only Son of the Heavenly Father, the Incarnate Word; on the other hand, it repeatedly states that Mary was truly His mother and allows us very naturally to conclude that she was therefore the Mother of God, the Mother of the Incarnate Word.[1] We shall examine each of these points briefly. Beginning with the divinity of Christ, we shall recall the principal texts that prove it beyond any possible doubt.

Jesus is True God

The Synoptic Gospels record the unheard-of claims that Christ made—that He was the true Son of God and equal to God. These Gospels then show Him justifying His claims by performing miracles. The literary form of the Gospels does not allow us to retrace the gradual progress of our Savior's teaching;[2] we cannot establish the time-sequence of the texts involved since they often follow only a logical order. But the atmosphere that prevailed in Christ's time, especially His audience's unpreparedness for the concept of several Persons in one divine nature, lead us to believe that His teaching must have been very gradual. If He had revealed too quickly and too clearly the mystery of His being a divine Person, He would simply have run the risk of being stoned as a blasphemer (cf. Lev. 24:16; John 8:59; 10:31).

Everyone admits that the direct power to forgive sins is the exclusive prerogative of God (Mark 2:5,7). Now Jesus claimed this power over the paralytic at Capharnaum and the repentant sinful woman who sought Him out in the house of Simon the Pharisee (Mark 2:5 ff.; Luke 7:48). He even regarded this power as being so much His very own that He delegated it to His Apostles (Matt. 16:18 f.; John 20:22 f.). In His Sermon on the Mount and in His discourse after the Last Supper, He spoke as the sovereign Law-giver who imparted to the divine commandments their definitive aspect (Matt. 5:17 ff.; John 13:34; 15:10). He never associated Himself with His hearers when He mentioned God the Father, never speaking of "our" Father but only of "my" Father and "your" Father (Luke 11:1; Matt. 10:29 ff.; John 20:17). Thus He allowed it to be understood that His Sonship was real and not simply adoptive. In the parable of the vine-dressers He represented Himself allegorically as the very son of the lord of the vineyard, whereas the prophets who had gone before Him were only servants (Matt. 12:1 ff.). As the Messias, the descendant of David, He claimed the prerogative of sitting at the right hand of God (Mark 12:35); and He declared to the members of the Great Sanhedrin that they would soon see that He did possess this prerogative (Matt. 26:64; John 19:7). The innate knowledge that He had of God the Father and that the Father had of Him was obviously inaccessible to anyone else except by means of revelation (Matt. 11:27).[3]

From beginning to end, the fourth Gospel also contains the same doctrine but stated even more boldly. Here, too, Christ continually referred to His pre-existence in Heaven. He existed before Abraham was (John 8:58); His own glory and His Father's love for Him existed before the creation of the world (John 17:5,24). Although He had come down from Heaven, He still remained there always and would soon ascend there again (John 3:13; 6:38,62; 8:33 f.; 20:17). Side by side with these allusions to His pre-existence, in the fourth Gospel Christ made many assertions that place Him on an equal level with God the Father. He said that as the Son He shared in the divine attributes, being Lord of the Sabbath, of life, of the resurrection and judgment (John 3:35; 5:17 ff.; 13:3; 16:16; 17:10). His equality with the Father is such that He is one with Him (John 10:30; 17:12), that He possesses everything that is the Father's (John 16:15; 17:10), and that He is in the Father and the Father in Him (John 14:9 ff.; 17:21). When He spoke of His dependence in relationship to the Father, it was because He regarded the Father as the Principle of His own divine life (John 5:26) and not because He was referring to a lower degree of divinity, which is logically an unthinkable concept. That, too, was the reason why He considered His human nature as completely subjected to the divine will (John 4:34; 6:38 ff.; 8:29,55; 14:10,31; 17:1 ff.).[4]

As an echo, or better still, as an extension of these Scripture texts, we must quote others that express the faith of the primitive Church in Christ's divinity. In his discourse shortly after Pentecost St. Peter spoke of Christ the man as the one whose prerogative it is to send the Holy Spirit; as the Lord of life, who sits at the right hand of God; as the Lord of all, the Judge of the living and the dead (Acts 2:33; 3:15; 5:31; 10:36,42). The dying St. Stephen called upon Him as one invokes God (Acts 7:59 f.). St. Paul wrote in his epistles that in Jesus dwells "all the fullness of the Godhead bodily," that He is the image of the invisible God, that He existed before every creative, that everything was created by Him and for Him (Col. 1:15 ff.; 2:9), that He is "God blessed forever," our great God and Savior (Rom. 9:5; Tit. 1:10; 2:13; cf. I Pet. 1:1), and that He deigned to take a body similar to ours in every way (Phil. 2:6 ff.). The author of the Epistle to the Hebrews was struck by wonder at the fact that God, having first spoken to us by the prophets, finally deigned to speak to us through His very own Son, Jesus, the Creator of all things, who is seated at the right hand of His Majesty (Hebr. I, 1–3). St. John himself wrote his Gospel to bring his readers to believe that Jesus is Christ, the Son of God (John 20:31). In fact, St. John is the theologian of the Incarnate Word, of the only Son who is in the bosom of the Father and who has made Him known to us (John 1:1 ff.; I John 1:1 ff.).

Mother of God

Only one conclusion can possibly be drawn from this array of Scripture texts—that Jesus was truly divine. That He also possessed human nature is a fact too evident to need emphasis, for His human nature was manifest from Bethlehem to Calvary. St. John, the most mystical of the New Testament writers, lays great stress upon it, showing us the Savior mingling with the guests at a wedding feast, suffering from fatigue and thirst at Jacob's well, using His spittle to cure the man born blind, weeping before the tomb of His friend Lazarus, washing His disciples' feet, and finally undergoing the torture of a horrifying Passion.

Our Lord's two natures did not form two persons but only one—that of the Word, the Son of God, as is clear from the Scripture texts in which He speaks of Himself (John 10:30; 14:10 ff.; 16:13 ff.; 17:9; etc.). This "self" is none other than that of the Person of the Word, who pre-existed from all eternity, who is unchangeable in Himself, and who at the Incarnation took on human nature. That is why the Apostles, in speaking of Christ, said that the Word was made flesh; that He dwelt among us; that He became like us in everything; that the Word of life, pre-existing from eternity, showed Himself to them by means of His Incarnation; that they had seen Him with their own eyes and touched Him with their hands; that men had crucified the Author of life; that God had purchased the Church with His own blood; that if "the rulers of this world" had really known the Lord of glory, they would never have crucified Him (John 1:14 ff.; Phil. 2:5 ff.; I John 1:1 ff.; Acts 3:15; 20:28; I Cor. 2:8). It follows that in Jesus there is only one Person, one divine existence, and that His human nature, with its operations, subsisted and existed only in a divine manner from the first moment of His conception.[5] This human nature is certainly real and individual, as even a glance at the Gospels shows; but it is not independent or autonomous. It was never, even for a moment, a new human person, because the Word was hypostatically united to it in creating it.

This is the Jesus whose mother was Mary. The angel had said to the Blessed Virgin: "Thou shalt conceive . . . a son and thou shalt give him the name Jesus"; and he had repeated this to Joseph: "She shall bring forth a son to whom thou shalt give the name Jesus." She did give birth to Jesus at Bethlehem, wrapping Him in swaddling clothes and laying Him in a manger. From then on, when the Gospels mention Jesus and Mary, they always call them the child and His mother (Matt. 2:11,13 f., 21; Luke 2:34,48,51); and to the very day of Pentecost, Mary's title remained "Mother of Jesus" (John 2:1,3,5; 19:25; Mark 3:31; Acts 1:14).

We can now state the conclusions we have reached on our subject. It goes without saying that, if we consider only the act of giving birth to a living being of flesh and blood, then Mary's motherhood was human and temporal, like that of all other women. But her motherhood was divine and transcended the mere act of becoming a mother because its object was the Word, in whom human nature exists and subsists. The objective of Mary's maternity was God, a Divine Person, and thus it established her in a unique relationship with God, in a mysterious personal relationship with the Incarnate Word. This relationship constitutes the essential element in the divine maternity, placing Mary above other creatures because no deeper relationship could exist between God and a human being.[6]

St. Thomas Aquinas says that, if we are not to fall into one or other of the many errors regarding Mary's maternity, we must first be as clear as possible on the mystery of Christ's humanity.[7] In the fifth century, Nestorius could see only a moral bond between the two natures in Christ. So he refused to grant Mary the title of Mother of God (*Theotókos*) because he wrongly imagined that it meant she was mother of the Godhead and that it made her a kind of goddess herself. We know the definition of the Council of Ephesus (431) on this matter: "If anyone does not confess that the Emmanuel is truly God, and, therefore, that the Virgin is truly the Mother of God, seeing that she begot according to the flesh the Word of God made flesh, let him be anathema."[8]

Notes

1. Cf. St. Thomas, *Summ. Theol.*, III, p. 35, a.4.
2. Cf. *Nouvelle Revue Théologique*, 1961, p. 25 ff., 31, art. by J. Levie.
3. Cf. *Lumière et Vie*, no. 9, Apr., 1953, *Jésus le Fils de Dieu*, p. 43 ff.; P. Benoit, *Exégèse et Théologie*, Paris, vol. 1, 1961, p. 117 ff.
4. Cf. Bardy-Tricot, *Le Christ*, Paris, 1935, p. 361 ff., 387 ff.; *Lumière et Vie, ibid.*, p. 101 ff.
5. Cf. *Maria*, vol. 6, p. 377.
6. Cf. *Maria*, vol. 6, p. 376 ff.; R. Laurentin, *Court Traité de Théologie Mariale*, Paris, 1959, p. 100 ff.; *Lumière et Vie*, no. 16, p. 43.
7. *Summ. Theol.*, III, Sent, dist, 4, q. 2, a. 2.
8. Denzinger-Bannwart, *Enchiridion Symbolorum*, 113.

12

The Visitation

The Gospel Text*

Now IN THOSE DAYS Mary arose and went with haste into the hill country,¹ to a town of Juda.² And she entered the house of Zachary and saluted Elizabeth. And it came to pass, when Elizabeth heard the greeting of Mary, that the babe in her womb leapt. And Elizabeth was filled with the Holy Spirit, and cried out with a loud voice, saying, "Blessed art thou among women and blessed is the fruit of thy womb! And how have I deserved that the mother of my Lord³ should come to me? For behold, the moment that the sound of thy greeting came to my ears, the babe in my womb leapt for joy. And blessed is she who has believed in the fulfillment of that which was said to her on the Lord's behalf.⁴ And Mary said: "My soul magnifies the Lord. . . ."

Departure

After the Annunciation Mary set out in haste across the mountain country of southern Palestine to a large village in Judea. The Evangelist does not mention the name of the village, which a tradition dating from the fifth century identifies with Ain Karim, nestling in a fertile valley at the foot of a barren mountain some four miles west of Jerusalem. She was going to visit her relative Elizabeth who six months before had been miraculously relieved of her sterility, which old age had apparently already made completely irreversible (Luke 1:7 ff.; 1:36). Mary did not yet know that Elizabeth would give birth to the Precursor of the Messias, for the angel had not made this point clear; but she soon learned about it because Zachary had been sufficiently informed on the matter during his vision in the Temple (Luke 1:15 ff.) and he had surely passed on the news to his wife by means of his writing tablets (Luke 1:63). No doubt this fact tightened the bonds of kinship between the two expectant mothers, a kinship the exact nature of which we cannot discern because the Greek text (Luke 1:36) leaves it vague.

At that period a young girl never traveled alone in Palestine, especially when the distance to be covered was great. In this case Mary had first to reach Jerusalem, eighty-seven miles south of Nazareth, before she turned west to Ain Karim. Her haste in setting out is not to be taken literally; instead, we should understand that she joined the first available caravan of pilgrims or traders going to the capital.

We can easily imagine her feelings as she traveled, for they were surely those which she soon expressed in the Magnificat. No doubt she praised God unceasingly for having deigned to cast His eyes upon her, effecting in her the wonders that would earn her the praise of all men.

Her departure had, of course, been inspired by the angel's

message. It practically invited her to go to Elizabeth so that, by verifying the work of God's power, she might banish all fear of having been deluded and experience a strengthening of confidence in God. The message had also given her to understand that in God's plan Elizabeth had to a certain extent the same destiny as she, and that therefore the two of them should share their common joy by meeting each other. Taking into account her kinswoman's age and condition, Mary had concluded that she should go to see Elizabeth rather than have the older woman come to see her. Thus she, the mother of Yahweh's Servant and the handmaid of the Lord, was the first one to announce the joyful tidings of the Gospel. "How beautiful upon the mountains," said the prophet, "are the feet of him who brings glad tidings . . . , announcing salvation, and saying to Sion, 'Your God is King!'" (Isa. 52:7).

Her journey, then, was not inspired by merely human motives—the natural longing to open her heart to someone, a desire to push herself forward, or a wish to assert herself— as is clearly shown by the attitude she adopted toward her intended husband, St. Joseph. She left home and returned after an absence of three months without saying a word to him about her condition; and neither the anguish he suffered (Matt. 1:19 ff.), of which she was aware, nor fear for her own fate, could induce her to speak. From the angel's silence about Joseph, she understood that God was reserving to Himself the duty of intervening in his regard, and she accepted as a prelude to the drama of redemption the suffering that accompanied her joy at the coming of the Messias.

Arrival

Mary was not long in receiving proof that she had properly interpreted the angel's message and that she could fearlessly trust in Providence during the whole course of events to come.

The customary greeting that she used when she met Elizabeth, "Peace be with thee," was in fact the occasion of several very significant supernatural events. Upon hearing this greeting, Elizabeth, filled with the Holy Spirit, understood that the sudden leap of the child in her womb was a leap of joy (cf. Luke 1:15); she realized that she was in the presence of an expectant mother who was incomparably blessed by God; she received a revelation that the young mother was carrying the Messias, her Lord (cf. Ps. 110:1); she was even informed about the faith which Mary had shown at the moment of the Annunciation (Luke 1:40-45). It is generally agreed that Elizabeth's words, "the mother of my Lord," simply meant "the mother of the Messias." Thus she gave the recently conceived Child one of the ancient royal titles, as the psalmist also had done (Ps. 110:1), and at the same time she stressed the fact that Mary had a dignity analogous to that of the Queen Mother (*gebirah*) in the time of the Hebrew monarchy.[5] Is the Evangelist here recalling a text from the Book of Samuel (2 Sam. 6:1 ff.) in order to compare Mary, carrying Jesus in her womb, to the Ark of the Covenant that David had caused to be borne through the land of Juda?[6] It is extremely unlikely that he is.

Our Lady did not have to tell Elizabeth about what had happened in Nazareth. God had already done this for her, giving her, at the same time, new proof of the reality of the Annunciation. He confirmed for her the greatness to which He had called her. In the presence of such greatness Elizabeth, like the angel, bowed down, for it was a greatness to which no other woman could aspire (cf. Judges 5:24; Jud. 13:18). He revealed to her one of the reasons for this greatness—her faith in the angel's message. Above all He gave her a better understanding of her son's incomparable majesty, which had brought her so much honor and was accompanied by so much divine power.

Even to us, all this suggests Mary's role as mediatrix, for "it was through her that we received the gift of the Messias and the graces connected with His coming" (A. Feuillet). Could she herself, then, have doubted even for a moment that God was watching over her with solicitude, that He was sheltering her under His love, and that what He wanted most from her was faith? We are not surprised, therefore, that she was so filled with grateful admiration that she longed to proclaim aloud the joy she felt and to give all praise and glory to God. In a moment we shall see the words with which she did so.

Mary, Model for Our Apostolate

Our Lady remained with Elizabeth for three months and did not return to Nazareth until after the birth and circumcision of the child, John the Precursor, when her help was no longer urgently needed.

Throughout this episode she was a model for our own apostolate. She teaches us that obedience and charity must be the foundations of our activity. She shows us that we must not keep those who need us waiting, even though they may not expect us; that we must face up to the difficulties involved, just as she did not hesitate before the journey of more than ninety miles over a mountain road; that we do not lower our dignity by serving others; that even in the midst of activity we can be recollected and can chant a Magnificat in our hearts; that we are always under the protection of Providence; that we sanctify our neighbor to the extent that we have Jesus within us; and that in our apostolate we are given confirmation of our faith, because in helping others we are helped ourselves.

Ancient Traditions

In the village of Ain Karim or Ein Karem ("the fountain of the vineyards"), four miles west of Jerusalem, stands the Franciscan monastery of St. John (the Baptist). The monastery church was probably built over the site of the house of Zachary and Elizabeth. In fact, from the fifth century down to our day a succession of religious monuments have been built here to honor the Precursor's birthplace. The Franciscans also have custody of another site which lies about five hundred yards farther west and on which stands the Church of the Visitation, with a small crypt that is built over the very spot on which Mary and Elizabeth met. Excavations made on this site in 1938 brought to light traces of medieval and Byzantine religious structures. Other locations, such as Jerusalem, Machaerus, Emmaus, Hebron and Bethzacharia, have sometimes been identified as the place where the Visitation occurred; but unlike Ain Karim, none of them possesses a very ancient tradition to support its claim.

The liturgical feast of the Visitation was one of the latest to be observed for it was not celebrated until the end of the thirteenth century. In 1389 Boniface IX extended the feast to the whole Church for the intention of ending the Great Western Schism.

Notes

1. The hill country was Judea, the highest region in all Palestine west of the Jordan.
2. We are not told the name of the town of the tribe of Juda, and it cannot be fixed with any certainty. It has been identified with several places—Ain Karim, Hebron, Yûttah and others.

3. The word Lord here means the Messias, whereas in verse 45 ("that which was said to her on the Lord's behalf . . ."), it means God.

4. As we have seen already (Chap. 10, note 4), the Vulgate translates this as "And blessed art thou who hast believed, because those things that were said to thee by the Lord shall be accomplished." Thus faith was not the reason why Mary was blessed.

5. Cf. R. de Vaux, *op. cit.*, vol. 1, p. 155–182.

6. Cf. R. Laurentin, *Luc I-II*, p. 79 ff.

13

Introduction to the Magnificat

The Name

IT IS CUSTOMARY in Catholic circles to give the name "Magnificat" to the canticle of thanksgiving which St. Luke puts on Mary's lips immediately after Elizabeth had praised her. The reason for the name is very simple. For many centuries the canticle was chanted in church in its Latin form only, beginning with the word *"magnificat"* ("My soul *magnifies*— that is, gives glory to or praises—the Lord"); hence it was natural that the first word should come to be used as the title for the whole canticle.

Translation

At the present day the English translation of the Magnificat is being used ever more widely even in religious functions. Here is a translation divided according to the meaning so as to allow us to follow more easily the subsequent developments (Luke 1:46–55*):

46 My soul magnifies the Lord,
47 and my spirit rejoices in God my Savior,
48 because he has cast his eyes on the lowliness of his handmaid. For, behold, henceforth all generations shall call me blessed,
49 because the Almighty has done great things for me, and holy is his name.
50 And his mercy extends from generation to generation upon those who fear him.
51 He has shown the strength of his arm.
He has scattered those who became proud in the thoughts of their hearts.
52 He has put down the mighty from their thrones but has raised up the lowly.
53 He has filled the hungry with good things but has sent the rich away with empty hands.
54 He has given help to Israel, his servant, remembering his mercy—
55 as he had promised our fathers—toward Abraham and his posterity forever.

Division

Those authors who have studied the rhythmical structure of the Magnificat are not in agreement as to the number of strophes it contains. Their estimates vary from two to five, but their disagreement is understandable when we remember that we possess only a Greek translation of the primitive Aramaic text.

If we take into account merely the thoughts expressed in the canticle, we see that, generally speaking, there are three principal parts. Without going into details, we shall review the ideas contained in each of these three sections.

The first (verses 46–49) expresses Mary's personal gratitude to God, who benignly granted her the ineffable favor of being the mother of the Messias and hence of being worthy of general admiration. The second part (vv. 50–53) reminds us that God had treated the humble Virgin in the same way in which He always treated the poor and humble, that is, those who, aware of their nothingness in this world, accept their condition and fill their hearts with the desire for divine things. The third part (vv. 54–55) specifies that the extraordinary favor which Mary had just received accomplished finally the biblical promises awaited by Abraham and his posterity.

Literary Background

The Magnificat is a veritable web of biblical allusions. In fact, it has been estimated that more than half the terms used in it were borrowed from the Old Testament. But the old scriptural texts are used and applied so evocatively that the finished canticle is by no means a mere combination of other people's words. Thus the phrases in the first part not only recall the joyful gratitude of Anna, the mother of Samuel, and of Lia, Jacob's wife, at the birth of their sons, but also show us that Mary's supernatural conception of Jesus was the ideal synthesis or climax of all the joyful births that went before. In the same way, by attributing to Mary the viewpoint of all the poor in spirit and by placing her at the moment in history when the messianic promises were fulfilled, the phrases in the other two parts of the Magnificat invite us to see in her a personification of the spirit of Israel taking possession of its long-awaited salvation.

This anthological character of the Magnificat, which is in close accord with the method employed in the context, allows us to grasp more perfectly the canticle's sweep of thought—from Mary, the eschatological personification of Israel, to the patriarch Abraham, the original personification of the Chosen People—including in its scope the whole Jewish nation that was, as it were, concentrated in them.[1]

Attributed to Mary

The Evangelist attributes the Magnificat to Mary and not to Elizabeth. All the existing copies of the primitive Greek text place the words: "And then Mary said . . ." at the beginning of the canticle, whereas only three ancient copies of a Latin translation of the text give Elizabeth's name here instead of Mary's, a variation that carries little weight and can be easily explained. All the ancient ecclesiastical writers, with only one exception, follow the reading of the primitive Greek text.

Furthermore, Mary's authorship of the canticle is much more in harmony with its contents and context than Elizabeth's would be; when we hold that our Lady composed it, it becomes part of a dialogue between her and her relative, corresponding to the angel's two preceding dialogues with Zachary and Mary herself. There is then an exact parallel between it and the Benedictus; each canticle was spoken by a person to whom the angel Gabriel had appeared, and each completed the account of the two related annunciations concerning the births of John the Baptist and of Christ.

In addition, it would have been most unbecoming and exaggerated for Elizabeth to have spoken her own praises and proclaimed that she was promised the admiration of all generations, when she had just bowed down and exalted the Mother of her Lord. But on the contrary, when Mary heard her cousin's praise she no doubt felt the need to give all the credit to God; and only she could have dreamed of receiving the admiration of future generations, because it was she who had been given a grace without equal. Again, she alone was able to see that this grace was the final stage in the history of the salvation, which had been promised since Abraham's time.

Elizabeth, too, obviously had reason to praise God, for He had miraculously put an end to her long-endured barrenness. Her situation, analogous to that of Anna, the mother of Samuel, gave her the right to draw inspiration from the Canticle of Anna to say: "I leap with joy in God my Savior, because he has cast his eyes on the *lowliness* of his handmaid" (1 Sam. 1:11; 2:1 ff.*). But she had already spoken her hymn of praise, and St. Luke has recorded it for us in its logical place, before the account of the Annunciation (Luke 1:25). It is very abbreviated in form, certainly, yet in it we see that when speaking of her barrenness, Elizabeth used the word "reproach." Like all the women of her land, she regarded childlessness as a disgrace (cf. Gen. 30–33) and even as a punishment (1 Sam. 1:5–8; 2 Sam. 6:23; Os. 9:11). But in her Magnificat Mary spoke only of her lowliness, her personal insignificance (Luke 1:48; cf. 1 Sam. 1:11; Ps. 30:8; Ecclus. 11:1,12).

Canticles of Thanksgiving in Israel

From time immemorial, wives in Israel used to express aloud the joy they felt at the prospect of bearing children. They regarded motherhood as the greatest blessing God could give them and the best safeguard of their easily destroyed married bliss. This was especially true in the case of those women who suffered from their husband's indifference, or who had been barren for many years and could no longer expect to have children. At the birth of Isaac, her first child, Sara, aged ninety, exclaimed: "God has given me cause for laughter, and whoever hears of it will laugh with me . . .

Who would have said to Abraham that Sara would nurse children? Yet I bore him a son in his old age" (Gen. 21:6–7). Lia, a rather neglected wife, regarded the children she bore as so many providential reasons for counting upon greater love from Jacob, her husband (Gen. 29:31 ff.). Rachel, who had been barren for a long time, praised God for having taken away her "reproach" when she gave birth to Joseph, her first-born son (Gen. 30:23). Anna, the mother of Samuel, could not contain her joy, when after long years of barrenness she finally gave birth to the future prophet. The canticle which the sacred writer puts on her lips on this occasion is the prototype of the Magnificat because it, too, praises the God of the humble and the lowly and ends by invoking the Messias-King (1 Sam. 2:1–10); but it is much less personal than Mary's canticle.

Again, when extraordinary favorable events occurred in Israel, they were regarded as the "wonders" of God (Exod. 3:20; 34:10; Jos. 3:5; Ps. 119:18; Job 5:9); and it was always the custom on such occasions to compose songs of thanksgiving. The most noted ones were the canticle that the Hebrews sang after passing through the Red Sea (Exod. 15:1 ff.), the Canticle of Moses before the Israelites entered the Promised Land (Deut. 32:1 ff.), that of Debora the prophetess after the victory over the Chanaanites (Judges 5:1 ff.), those of King Ezechias, the Books of Habacuc, Judith and Daniel (Isa. 38:10 ff.; 26:1 ff.; Hab. 3; Judith 16:1 ff.; Dan. 3:52 ff.), and especially those of the psalmists David, Asaph, and others. These canticles and psalms of thanksgiving became classical after the Babylonian Exile. They were used in public worship and private life whenever thanks was to be given to God.[2]

Like the canticles of the aged Simeon and the priest Zachary (Luke 1:67 ff.; 2:29 ff.), the Magnificat was inspired by these customs and literary types. Mary had more reason than anyone before her to proclaim the praises of God, for no other women had had a son like hers; and the marvel that had been accomplished in her was the greatest of God's "wonders."

Notes

1. Cf. R. Laurentin, *Luc I-II*, p. 85.
2. Cf. Robert-Feuillet, *Introduction à la Bible* (Paris, 1959), vol. 1, p. 596 ff.; P. Drijvers, *Les Psaumes, genres litteraires et thèmes doctrinaux* (Paris, 1958), p. 83 ff.

14

Explanation of the Magnificat

God's Goodness to Mary

As was most natural, Mary began her canticle by praising God on her own account (Luke 1:46–49). Indeed, she herself was the greatest beneficiary of God's goodness. "My soul magnifies the Lord, and my spirit rejoices in God my Savior," she said, perhaps remembering the psalmists who called upon others to "magnify" the Lord with them (Ps. 34:4; 69:31), whose souls rejoiced in Yahweh and were jubilant in His salvation (Ps. 35:9). Or perhaps she was thinking rather about the Canticle of Anna, the mother of Samuel, which begins with the words "My soul exults in Yahweh"; or about the passage from the prophet Habacuc that says: "Yet will I rejoice in Yahweh and exult in God my Savior (3:18*). We do know that Mary used Hebrew turns of phrase and modes of thought. Thus instead of saying "I glorify God and I rejoice," as a westerner would, she used two synonyms, "my soul" and "my spirit," in place of the personal pronoun; and instead of expressing her thought in one phrase as we would have done, she repeated it twice, using the device of synonymous parallelism—each repetition adding different nuances. First, she proclaimed the greatness of God as Lord and Sovereign Ruler; then she expressed her great joy in the God of Israel, in Yahweh the Savior, the Author of deliverance. In calling God her Savior, she was thinking of the messianic salvation which had been promised in the Old Testament and which at long last was finally begun by the coming of Jesus the Messias. Zachary and the aged Simeon would also bless God, at the coming of Jesus, for the messianic salvation bestowed (Luke 1:68 f.; 2:30). Even though Mary had been preserved from original sin, she could still call God her Savior; we must not forget that it was by the application of the future merits of her son that she had been granted her Immaculate Conception.[1]

Mary had good reason to praise God in this way on her own account, as she herself explained when she came to reveal her motives: "I exalt the Lord . . . , because he has cast his eyes on the lowliness of his handmaid" (cf. 1 Sam. 1:11; Ps. 31:8). In biblical language "to cast one's eyes on someone, to regard someone" meant to show benevolence to someone in a concrete manner, while "to turn one's eyes away from someone" meant to punish him in one way or another. Hence our Lady was exultant and rejoiced because she had been favored by God. Obviously, she was singularly aware of the great honor done her at the Annunciation; but at the same time she was conscious of the absolutely gratuitous nature of that honor. She acknowledged her lowliness, or, as we would say today, her worthlessness, her spiritual poverty, and her nothingness before God.[2] She claimed for herself only the position of a "handmaid," that is, a humble worshipper of God, as she had done at the very moment of the Annunciation (Luke 1:38). Her sentiments and the words which she used to express them are similar to those of the psalmist who cried out: "O God of truth, you hate those who worship vain idols, but my trust is in Yahweh; I exult in and rejoice at your love. You have seen my nothingness . . . , and you have allowed me to move about at large" (Ps. 31:7 ff.*). Our Lady spoke of her lowliness as Anna, the mother of Samuel, spoke of hers when she begged God to give her a son (1 Sam. 1:11). For Mary, as for all the poor in spirit of the Old Testament, there was no greatness except in God, no recourse except to Him; for only Yahweh can remedy the innate poverty of men's nature.

Mary was fully aware that by God's grace she had gone from poverty to riches, and she saw that she had been more highly favored than any other women in the world could ever be: "Henceforth all generations shall call me blessed, because the Almighty has done great things for me." She foresaw the incomparable glory that would be hers as mother of the Messias. From then on, her name and that of her son would not be separated, as Elizabeth had indicated to her: "Blessed art thou among women and blessed is the fruit of thy womb." Many years later an admirer of the Gospel message was to be among the first women to prove the truth of these words by including Mary in the praise she gave Jesus: "Blessed is the womb that bore thee, and the breasts that nursed thee" (Luke 11:27). It is true that in Israel every mother regarded herself as blessed, and expected to be congratulated by her neighbors when she gave birth to a son (cf. Gen. 30:13); but only Mary could predict that she would receive the felicitations of every generation. And she would owe this future happiness, also, to God who had done great things for her, wonders such as those He had wrought before (Ps. 71:19; 105:21). Modestly she forgot that she would owe it also to her faith, as Elizabeth, at the inspiration of the Holy Spirit, had pointed out to her. Here, when speaking of God, Mary called Him "the Almighty" because He had done great things; when she added "and holy is his name," she was following the Semitic custom of using a laudatory phrase after any mention of the divine name—a tradition to which St. Paul was very faithful (cf. Rom. 1:25). The phrase that Mary used recalls that of the psalmist (Ps. 111:9), and acknowledges that God transcends the secular world (cf. Isa. 6:1 ff.). In fact, in biblical language the divine *name* designates God Himself, while His *holiness* indicates His separation from the secular world.[3]

God's Goodness to the Humble
(Luke 1:50–53)

In the second part of her Magnificat (Luke 1:50–53), our Lady attributed to God's mercy the favor she had received and the happiness that would be hers as a result. She declared that the divine mercy, made up of compassion, pity, goodness, and tenderness,[4] extends from age to age upon those who fear God. Here she borrowed two expressions from the psalmist (Ps. 103:17), identifying those who fear God as "those who keep his covenant and remember to do his will" (*ibid.* v. 18*). Indirectly she hereby told us that she was one of those "who hear the word of God and keep it" (Luke 11:28), as Christ would say later; for she more than anyone else was the object of the divine mercy. In this respect her kinswoman had marked out the way for her, to judge by what the Gospel says about Zachary and Elizabeth: "Both were just in the eyes of God and they followed fault-

lessly all the commandments and ordinances of the Lord"
(Luke 1:6*).

Returning to the parallelism which she used in the beginning (46–47) but employing antithesis now (52–53) instead of synonyms (51), Mary contrasted God's mercy with
His avenging justice. Here she made use of the ancient
anthropomorphic terminology of Israel to describe the way
in which God exercises His justice: "He has shown the
strength of his arm (cf. Ps. 89:11). He has scattered those
who became proud in the thoughts of their hearts." We can
readily see what our Lady meant if we remember that in
ancient Hebrew psychology the heart was the seat of desires
and thoughts: God shows His avenging might by reducing
to nothingness those who, far from doing His will, defy Him
with their self-sufficiency and pretensions to independence.
Having stated this principle, Mary demonstrated its application, as it were. She depicted two types of the proud who were
overtaken by divine justice, and she contrasted them with
two classes of God's servants who received the benefits of
His mercy—the powerful and the rich on one hand, the
lowly and the hungry on the other. The elements in this
tableau also come from the Old Testament (Job 12:19; 5:11;
Ps. 107:9), where the device of reversing roles is classical.
Later, our Lord would point out the dangers of power and
riches, and he would extol the spirit of poverty; for power and
wealth easily lead to self-satisfaction, whereas the spirit of
poverty predisposes us to humility. No matter what some
authors may say,[5] it is improbable that Mary was referring
to usurpers of David's throne when she spoke about the
mighty being put down (v. 52); the parallelism of the context does not lend itself easily to such an interpretation. But
when she mentioned filling the hungry and sending the
rich away with empty hands, she was referring to the cus-

tomary practice at oriental courts of admitting only the rich. One of the marks of the messianic kingdom would be solicitude for the poor (Isa. 61:1; Luke 4:18; 7:22) and for raising up those who humble themselves (Luke 14:11; 18:14).

God's Goodness to Israel
(Luke 1:54–55)

In the third part of her Magnificat Mary showed that the grace she had received at the Annunciation was the realization of the promises made to the ancestors of Israel regarding Abraham and his posterity. By bringing about the conception of the Messias, God had "given help to Israel, his servant, remembering his mercy" (cf. Ps. 98:3; Isa. 41:8 f.). Precisely because the main body of the Chosen People had remained God's "servant," faithfully keeping His laws and being obedient to His will, they were now benefiting from His mercy, which extends from age to age upon those who fear Him (cf. Luke 1:50). The coming of the Messias was the supreme expression of that mercy, which had been exercised so many times in the past; yet Christ's coming was simply the fulfillment of the promise made to the "fathers" (cf. Luke 1:54), that is, to the ancestors of the Chosen People. This was a clear reference to the many messianic promises of the Old Testament, which had been made more and more precise as the centuries passed, but without ever being understood perfectly.[6] As we read in Genesis, the promises had been made in favor of Abraham and his posterity (Gen. 12:3; 13:15; 22:18), and for the moment Mary was perhaps thinking only of the Jewish people. But soon our Lord, and later St. Paul, would show that the promises had been made to Abraham as the father of believers and of all those who, whether they were Jews or not, would be his spiritual sons, the heirs to his faith (John 8:37 ff.; Rom. 4:1 ff.; Matt. 3:9). The last word in the Magnificat, "forever," indicates that the coming of the Messias was to establish once for all, God's mercy on the "Israel," that is, on the "chosen nation," of believers (cf. Gal. 4:28; 6:15). We should note in passing that Greek grammar forbids us to translate the last two verses of the Magnificat as "He has given help to Israel, his servant, remembering his mercy, as he said to our fathers, Abraham and his posterity," because "Abraham" is in the dative case and hence must be dependent upon the verb "remembering" and not upon "said."

Conclusion

From beginning to end of this beautiful Marian poem, our Lady's soul shines through the themes she chose from the past. Her humility, that is, her complete self-abandonment to God, illuminates them, raising them to heights which they had never attained before. Without seeking it, she became the ideal personification of God's people journeying toward the Messias. In her were realized all the promises that had begun in the time of Abraham, the father of the servants of God, and so she stood at the meeting place of the two Israels, the ancient and the new.

Notes

1. Cf. J. J. Weber, *op. cit.*, p. 44; Bossuet, *Sermon du 8 décembre 1656*.
2. Cf. A. Gelin, *Les Pauvres de Yahvé* (Paris, 1953), p. 127 ff.
3. Cf. P. Van Imschoot, *Théologie de l'Ancien Testament*, Paris, 1954, vol. 1, p. 43 ff.
4. Cf. *Vocabulaire de Théologie Biblique*, Paris, 1962, p. 626 ff.
5. Cf. M. J. Lagrange, *Evangile selon saint Luc*, Paris, 1925, p. 49.
6. Cf. DBS, article on "Messianisme," pp. 1165–1212.

15

Our Lady's Marriage

*The Gospel Text**

Now THE ORIGIN of Christ was in this wise. When Mary his mother had been betrothed to Joseph, she was found, before they came together, to be with child by the Holy Spirit. But Joseph her (future) husband, being a just man, and not wishing to expose her to reproach was minded to put her away privately. But while he thought on these things, behold, an angel of the Lord appeared to him in a dream, saying, "Do not be afraid, Joseph, son of David, to take to thee Mary thy (future) wife, for that which is begotten in her is of the Holy Spirit. And she shall bring forth a son, and thou shalt give him the name Jesus, because he shall save his people from their sins." Now all this came to pass that there might be fulfilled what was spoken by the Lord through the prophet, saying, "Behold, the virgin shall be with child, and shall bring forth a son; and they shall call his name Emmanuel"; which is, interpreted, "God with us." So Joseph, arising from sleep, did as the angel of the Lord had commanded him and took his betrothed into his house. And, without his having known her,[1] she brought forth a son.[2] And he called his name Jesus.

Joseph's Ordeal

When Mary returned from visiting her cousin Elizabeth, she resumed her normal life in Nazareth, waiting until her fiancé could gather the customary bride-money and the usual gifts.[3] Every day on her way to draw water, she was able to see him in his workshop near the fountain. Only since the seventeenth century has the name "Joseph's Workshop" been given to a cave that lies a mere hundred yards or so north of the traditional site of the Annunciation.

Soon the preliminary signs of her approaching maternity became evident and, naturally, they did not escape Joseph, who was astounded and distressed as a result. What was he to do? He could have invoked the law, since the legal effects of Jewish betrothal were similar to those of marriage. An engaged girl who was suspected of voluntary infidelity to her fiancé was publicly denounced in the local court; and if the accusations of at least two witnesses were sufficiently well-founded, she was condemned to death by stoning. Even when there was no case against her, the very fact that she had been summoned before the court did her reputation no good; and although she might simply be the innocent victim of a carnal assault, she still ran the risk of being repudiated by her fiancé. In the event of repudiation the procedure was very discreet and took place in the privacy of the home, where, in writing and in the presence of two witnesses, she was given liberty to leave her fiancé for another man. She suffered no injury to her reputation because in those days the grounds for divorce were often extremely trivial and, in any case, were not written into the bill of repudiation. When the circumstances arose, injured pride undoubtedly caused many young fiancés to forget legal niceties and rush to take the severest measures. But Joseph, a just man himself, had too much respect for justice to deliver Mary over to the court. Because of her obvious holiness, he could only conclude that, at most, she had been the unwilling victim of a deplorable incident; and so he resolved to have recourse to simple repudiation (Matt. 1:19), which at that time left every door open to the young woman concerned.

Divine Intervention

Then Providence intervened. One night, perhaps the very eve of Joseph's carrying out his decision regarding Mary, an angel appeared to him in a dream and told him of what God had brought about in his betrothed: "That which is begotten in her is of the Holy Spirit." The angel counseled him to marry his fiancée: "Do not be afraid . . . to take Mary into thy house," and told him to act officially as father of the child by naming Him: "Thou shalt give him the name Jesus." Finally, the angel partially revealed the child's spiritual, saving destiny: "He shall save his people from their sins" (Matt. 1:20–21*).

A noted commentator on Scripture has suggested that St. Joseph's actions and God's intervention should be interpreted in another way. Here, in brief, is his theory.[4] Joseph had previously been informed about the circumstances of Mary's pregnancy, so that when the angel appeared to him, he already knew that she had conceived of the Holy Spirit, as the beginning of the Gospel account leads the reader to

understand: "She was found . . . to be with child by the Holy
Spirit" (Matt. 1:18). And that was precisely the reason why
he was going to leave Mary, for he had concluded that God
did not want the proposed marriage to take place and that
He had reserved to Himself the right of assuring the future of
His chosen handmaid. Joseph, then, had resolved to withdraw from the scene; but with the sensitivity and tact which
were part of his "justice" toward God, he had decided not
to *divulge* the mystery to anyone. It was at this point that
the angel appeared to the young man, officially assured him
of Mary's virginal conception, told him to take Mary into
his house nevertheless, and showed him that the reason
for this demand was to make him, who was a descendant of
David, the adoptive father of the child. This theory, the
author says, is based on the following translation of the
angel's message in the Gospel: "Therefore, Joseph, do not
be afraid to take to thee Mary . . . for *without doubt* (*gár*)
that which is begotten in her is of the Holy Spirit, *but* she
shall bring forth a son, and thou shalt give him the name
Jesus" (Matt. 1:20). And actually, the author continues,
Joseph did go on to act as a foster father, marrying Mary and
naming the child (Matt. 1:23,25). However, the weakness
in this theory is that it depends completely on giving a
particular shade of meaning to a simple conjunction (*gár*).

The angel's announcement to Joseph fully confirmed the
one made to Mary and even completed it on one point. The
reference to the work of the Holy Spirit emphasized the
virginal conception (Luke 1:35), while the mention made
of Joseph's descent from David and of his legal paternity
of the child recalled the fact that Jesus would inherit the
throne of David, His father (Luke 1:32). A third reference
which the angel made was also a reminder of the Child's
royalty, for Israel would be *His* people; but the saving,

spiritual nature of His kingship was specified—He would save His people from their sins.

It is not difficult to imagine the joy Joseph felt upon awakening from his dream, for it shines through the Gospel text, where his haste to obey God's wishes is stressed: "So Joseph, arising from sleep, did as the angel of the Lord had commanded him, and took his betrothed (into his house)." When Mary learned about this second angelic announcement she must have found it another reason for singing about the wonders of God. She drew from it a greater trust in divine providence, which was able to achieve its ends at just the right moment. Now she understood better that the anguish which she and Joseph had suffered as they endured their seemingly endless uncertainty, had been willed by God for their advancement in holiness.[5]

The Marriage

As soon as possible after the angel's message, the wedding ceremonies were organized (Matt. 1:24). With a nuptial crown on his head the bridegroom, accompanied by his friends and a group of musicians, went to Mary's house. There she awaited him in her festive garments, wearing her modest store of jewelry, with her face veiled, and surrounded by her friends. Then with songs and music the young bride was joyfully brought in procession to Joseph's house, where the essential part of the ceremony took place—the bride's solemn entry into the bridegroom's dwelling. Then followed a feast which lasted for several days at least.[6]

This true marriage, begun in perfect chastity (Luke 1:34; Matt. 1:20), was never to cast a shadow on Mary's virginity, and it is completely erroneous to interpret the Gospel text as implying the contrary: "And (Joseph) did not know her till she had brought forth her firstborn son" (Matt. 1:25).

Here the verb "to know" has the Semitic meaning of having conjugal relations; but, more important, the adverb "till," as in several other biblical passages (e.g., Gen. 8:7; Ps. 110:1), refers only to the past and not to the future. Thus it was said of Michol, one of David's wives, that she had no child till the day of her death (2 Sam. 6:23*). We ourselves use similar expressions; for example, we say that a hardened criminal remained unrepentant *till* death, or that someone died *before* carrying out all his plans. Hence the text in question simply means to corroborate the virginal conception of Christ, already mentioned (Matt. 1:18,20). It attests that Christ's birth was independent of any conjugal relation; and the whole Gospel account has the same purpose in view.

It is a misuse of language to take the conjunction "till" in a restrictive sense and as referring to the future; some authors do,[7] remembering "the brethren (brothers)" of Jesus mentioned later (John 2:12; 7:5; Mark 3:20f., 31ff.; 6:2f.; Acts 1:14). This interpretation forgets the sole purpose of the Gospel passage and gives the phrase "the brethren of Jesus" an absolute value that it does not possess in the Gospels. The phrase simply refers to our Lord's *cousins*, as we shall realize with a little thought. Jesus alone is called *the* son of Mary during His public ministry (Mark 6:3). Only He accompanied Mary and Joseph on their annual pilgrimages to Jerusalem (Luke 2:41ff.), and on at least two occasions (Mark 3:20f.; John 7:3ff.) His "brethren" treated Him as a junior, and not as the eldest member of their family. Again, He would never have given His mother into St. John's care as He hung on the cross if He had had brothers in the strict sense of the term (John 19:25f.); to do so would have been to go against all the accepted customs of the day. And on Calvary Mary was accompanied by the mother of two of those who had been called his "brothers"

(Mark 15:50; 6:2 ff.). The fact is that even today in Semitic languages the word "brother" has a much wider meaning than in the European languages, including as it does brothers strictly so called, step-brothers, nephews, cousins, relatives in general, and even mere compatriots. That is why we should consider the texts as a whole, and not be put out of stride by an occasional verse that is apparently more difficult than the others.

Many manuscripts give the last verse of this chapter as "And, without his having known her, she brought forth her *firstborn* son" (Matt. 1:25). As we have already implied, it is possible that these manuscripts were influenced by the text describing the Nativity in which we read, "Mary . . . brought forth her firstborn son . . . ." (Luke 2:7). When we come to deal with the Nativity, we shall see that there is nothing surprising about the Evangelist's use of the term "firstborn" to describe the child Jesus.

Notes

1. The literal translation is: "He did not know her *until* she had brought forth a son." This text simply stresses the fact that Mary was a virgin at Christ's birth. It is not concerned with later developments which the rest of the Gospel and tradition were to deal with.
2. The majority of the manuscripts have "her *firstborn* son." See Luke 2:7: "And she brought forth her firstborn son . . . , and laid him in a manger. . . ."
3. Cf. R. de Vaux, *op. cit.*, vol. 1, p. 48 ff.
4. The theory is expounded in *Mélanges Bibliques en l'honneur de André Robert*, ed. by Boud and Gay (Paris, 1957), pp. 390–397. It was written by Fr. Xavier Léon-Dufour, S. J. and is entitled: "*L'Annonce à Joseph.*" Cf. P. Gächter, *Maria im Erdenleben*, Innsbruck, 3rd ed., 1955, p. 113 ff.
5. Cf. Jean Galot, *Saint Joseph*, Desclée de Brouwer, 1962, p. 27 f.
6. Cf. R. de Vaux, *op. cit.*, vol. 1, p. 58 ff.
7. Cf. V. Taylor, *The Gospel According to St. Mark* (London, 1952), p. 247 ff.

16

Joseph and Mary

The Villager of Nazareth

IN ACCORDANCE with the customs of his people, Joseph had been circumcised and given his name on the eighth day after his birth (Gen. 17:10; Lev. 19:23; Luke 2:21). The name he received was that of an illustrious ancestor, Jacob's son, who had been sold into slavery by his brothers and had risen to become the chief minister of the Pharaoh of Egypt (Gen. 37–50). As the reader will remember, Jacob's wife Rachel had named her first son Joseph (which means "May [He] add [another son]!") because she wished to become a mother again (Gen. 30:23). Besides bearing a great name, Joseph of Nazareth was of royal lineage, being descended from the ancient family of David. As we have already seen, the Evangelists stress this fact several times, especially in the two genealogical lists of Christ's ancestors (Matt. 1:1 ff.; Luke 3:23; cf. Matt. 1:20; Luke 1:27; 2:4).

Joseph was no doubt born in Nazareth and not in Bethlehem, the country of his ancestors. In fact, it seems that no one in Bethlehem even remembered any of his closer relatives, because he could find no place to stay when he went there for the census. Despite his royal descent, he was poor; but this is not surprising because descent from David had then lost much of its prestige. So many centuries had passed since the kings of Juda had reigned, that the heirs of the dynasty then probably numbered thousands. Joseph accordingly had never known any home other than one of the wretched dwellings in Nazareth, which were mere mud huts built on the hillside, containing only one room, rectangular in shape, and sometimes stretching back into a small cave in the rear. Recent excavations have unearthed traces of these houses, as we noted when speaking about the Annunciation.

Like all the boys of his country and era, at about the age of five Joseph must have gone to the teacher at the synagogue to be taught to read the sacred texts. From the age of thirteen he would have had to learn a trade and obey all the prescriptions of the Jewish religion. He was unusually zealous in following out these prescriptions, for, as the Scriptures tell us, he even earned the reputation of being a *just* man (Matt. 1:19), that is, a faithful follower of God's will (cf. Luke 1:6). St. Luke notes particularly that he took part in the Passover pilgrimage to Jerusalem every year (Luke 2:41). He was a carpenter by trade (Matt. 13:55), that is to say, he worked in wood and iron, making all the objects necessary for tilling the fields and building houses. St. Justin, speaking about the carpentry trade as followed by our Lord (cf. Luke 6:3), tells us that He made ploughs and yokes.[1]

Joseph's trade, which placed him at the mercy of his

clients, did not make him rich, to judge by the meager offering he was able to make at Mary's Purification (Luke 2:24). Since a trade passed from father to son, we can suppose that his family's fortunes had not been bright for a long time past. What was his father's name? We do not know for certain. The genealogical lists mention Jacob (Matt. 1:16) and Heli (Luke 3:23) without making it clear whether or not they are both dealing with one and the same person. The lists do not even give us a clue as to whether they are concerned with natural or with legal paternity. The only detail that we know about Joseph's family was supplied at quite a later date by Eusebius of Caesarea. He quotes Hegesippus to the effect that Cleophas, whose wife stood with Mary on Calvary (John 19:25), was Joseph's brother.[2] Perhaps this piece of information may help toward clearing up the question of our Lord's "brothers" or "brethren."[3]

Spouse of the Virgin Mary

In Israel, when a young man had learned a trade and was on the threshold of adult life, he began to think about marriage, usually about the age of eighteen. In fact, according to the manuscripts found in Qumrân near the Dead Sea, those members of the Essene sect who married were forbidden to wait beyond the age of twenty before doing so. Joseph followed the general practice of his time, and Mary became his betrothed (Luke 1:26) after discussions between their two families about the marriage settlement or *mohar*. The betrothal was made official by a formula pronounced over Joseph by his father-in-law or someone representing him: "Today thou shalt be my son-in-law." From that moment on, the young man and woman were united by legal bonds which were analogous to those of marriage but which are unknown, however, in our culture.[4]

As we have seen, voluntary celibacy was not common among Joseph's contemporaries; and even the Essenes did not demand it of all the members of their sect. According to the more usual interpretation of Mary's reply to the angel Gabriel at the Annunciation ("How shall this be done, since I do not know man?") it seems indisputable that Joseph, at least when he had become betrothed to Mary and had learned about her virginal resolve, approved of and shared fully in it. His pained astonishment upon learning that Mary was expecting a child shows his personal chastity and his ignorance of God's plans for him. His decision not to bring his betrothed before the local court, but to place in her hands a bill of divorce that would set her free, is a proof of his uprightness in legal matters and of his conviction that Mary was completely innocent. As we have said, only those girls who were suspected of having been voluntarily unfaithful to their fiancés could be brought before the local court; and even when they were exonerated their reputation was ever afterwards somewhat tainted. His haste to take Mary as his wife, to bring her ceremoniously into his home as his bride when he had been supernaturally informed about the mystery of the Incarnation, shows the tender affection he had for her and his full, willing consent to God's plans once he knew them. He was happy to be able to shelter the virginal fecundity of the Mother of God under the veil of a pure and holy marriage. Thanks to him, the reputation of the most innocent of creatures would not be compromised even for a moment. He understood now more than ever how Mary's virginal resolve had been inspired from on high: "God had willed to keep her for Himself so as to make her a mother."[5]

Apocryphal accounts have popularized the legend of Joseph as being a widower well-advanced in years and the father of many children when Mary was confided to his care. The later legends describe him as being ninety years old at the time of the Annunciation and 111 years when he died.[6] In their eagerness to find some natural explanation for a mystery that eludes their grasp, the legends contradict the Gospels on a number of points. They shift the scene to the very temple in Jerusalem, in the presence of the High Priest, instead of placing it in Nazareth and within the intimacy of the family circle. They give Joseph merely the role of a temporary guardian and not a true husband; and they supply him with several children by a previous marriage; whereas our Gospels, in circumstances that would require it, make no mention of such children—as we have seen.

Father of Jesus

According to the religious law of his nation, Joseph, by his marriage to Mary, became the legal father of the child Jesus and passed on to Him all his prerogatives of race and ownership. God acknowledged this right by commanding Joseph to name the child on the day of His circumcision (Matt. 1:21; Luke 2:21) and by telling him to take the measures necessary for safeguarding the child when Herod and his successor menaced His life (Matt. 2:19–22). This is the law to which Mary and the Evangelists were referring when they called Joseph the father of Jesus (Luke 2:48; 4:22; John 6:42), as were the genealogical lists when they established Christ's descent from David through Joseph (Matt. 1:1 ff.; Luke 3:23 ff.).

We can guess the care with which Joseph performed his duties as Christ's legal father. The Gospels provide us with sufficient detail for that, telling us how he did everything possible in the arduous circumstances of the Nativity; paid to the Temple the redemption fee required at the birth of every firstborn son; took the child out of the dangers that threatened His life; accustomed Him to the annual observance of the Jewish feasts (Luke 2:41 ff.) as well as to weekly attendance at the synagogue (Luke 4:16); sought Him anxiously for three days along with Mary, when He stayed behind in Jerusalem; was obeyed by Him (Luke 2:51); initiated Him into everything that favored His growth in wisdom, stature and grace (Luke 2:40,52); and taught Him his own trade as a carpenter (Luke 6:3).

Joseph carried out his duties as legal father so thoroughly and prudently that all his compatriots, even those in Nazareth, thought that Jesus was his real son (Luke 4:22; Matt. 13:55); they did not know about the virginal conception. God permitted it to be that way because He did not wish Christ's greatness to be revealed prematurely. We know that our Savior Himself had to show who He was and teach His doctrine very gradually because of the Jewish preconceptions about the nature and role of the Messias. Hence, practically speaking, Joseph had among other duties the task of arranging the transitions in the mystery of the Incarnation. Naturally this work ended the moment Christ's public ministry began, because all ambiguity of expression had to cease when our Lord commenced to speak about His heavenly Father. Therefore, we need not be surprised to find that Joseph is not mentioned in the Gospels after that time. God must have already taken him to Himself; otherwise we could not explain his absence from the group of relatives who came to stop Jesus from preaching for reasons of health (Mark 3:20 ff.); nor could we understand our Lord's action on the cross when He confided His mother to St. John who, after all, was only a disciple; and it would be hard to see why Joseph's name does not figure in the list of those who waited with Mary for the coming of the Holy Spirit at Pentecost (Acts 1:14).[7]

The Saint

God bestows His graces on His saints in accordance with the functions He wishes them to perform. Joseph was given the highest possible function, Mary's spouse and Christ's legal father. It follows, then, that God gave him the rarest and most abundant graces. This, and not advanced age, is the explanation of his virginal marriage. We have tried to see how perfectly he corresponded with all God's wishes. The long years he spent close to Jesus and Mary lead us to believe that his original sanctity must have increased extraordinarily up to the very moment of his death. To say the least, it would be a slur on this sanctity and would show ignorance of the power of grace, to maintain that brothers and sisters of Jesus were born into the Holy Family after the Incarnation. As we have said, the Gospel texts, properly understood, are opposed to this view.

The Church delayed a long time in declaring the sanctity of Joseph. The first important papal pronouncements that all Christians should solemnly venerate the head of the Holy Family date back only to Sixtus IX (1471–1484). Devotion to St. Joseph was emphasized more strongly in the seventeenth and eighteenth centuries by Gregory XV (May 8, 1621), Clement X (Dec. 6, 1670), Clement XI (Feb. 4, 1714), and Benedict XIII (Dec. 19, 1726), but it reached much greater heights from the reign of Pius IX onward. At a time when the forces of evil were uniting against Christianity, the holy Pontiff turned to Joseph, the head of the Holy Family— the Church in embryo—and proclaimed him Patron of the Universal Church by the decree *Quemadmodum Deus* (December 8, 1870). Since then we have been given the masterly encyclical by Leo XIII on the foundations of devotion to St. Joseph (Aug. 15, 1889); the *Motu Proprio* of Benedict XV naming him the Patron of workers (July 25, 1920); the decree of Pius XII making May 1 the Feast of St. Joseph, Patron of Workers (May 1, 1955); and the decision of the late Holy Father, John XXIII, to inscribe the name of Joseph after that of Mary in the Canon of the Mass (Nov., 1962).[8]

With the Church we venerate and invoke this great saint who is also the patron of vocations and a happy death. But in our devotions we should never separate him from Jesus and Mary. Let us ask him to watch over us as he once watched over the Holy Family; to make us see every human being as one who has been called to become a brother of Christ and a son of Mary;[9] to teach us the value of renunciation, devotion, purity, recollection, and work; to obtain for us the grace of final perseverance under the benevolent gaze of Jesus and Mary.

Notes

1. St. Justin, *Dialogue with Trypho*, 88. Cf. The apocryphal *Gospel of Thomas*, chap. 13; see *Biblica*, 1923, pp. 41–55.

2. Eusebius, *Hist. Eccles.*, III, 11, and IV, 22, 4.

3. Cf. *Recherches des Sciences Religieuses*, 1927, pp. 127–138; F. Prat, *Jesus Christ*, tr. by J. J. Heenan, S. J., Bruce (Milwaukee, 1950) p. 132 ff.; D. Buzy, *Evangile selon S. Matthieu*, Paris, 1946, p. 166; Lagrange, *Evangile de Jésus-Christ*, p. 281.

4. Cf. R. de Vaux, *op. cit.*, vol. 1, p. 57 ff.

5. J. Galot, *Saint Joseph*, Desclée de Brouwer (Paris, 1962), p. 32 f.

6. Cf. *Histoire de Joseph le Charpentier*, chap. 14; *Protoevangelium of James*, chaps. 9–16. See F. Filas, *The Man Nearest to Christ*, Bruce, Milwaukee, 1944, p. 19 ff.

7. Cf. J. Galot, *op. cit.*, p. 149 ff.

8. Cf. F. Filas, *op. cit.*, p. 195 ff.

9. Cf. J. Galot, *op. cit.*, p. 42: "(Joseph) helps Christians to take Mary into their homes, to give her a prominent place in their thoughts and feelings. . . . Above all, he helps (us) . . . to share the Blessed Virgin's ideals."

17

The Birth of Christ

Now it came to pass in those days, that there went forth a decree from Caesar Augustus that a census of the whole world should be taken. This first census took place while Cyrinus was governor of Syria.¹ And all were going, each to his own town, to register. And Joseph also went from Galilee out of the town of Nazareth into Judea to the town of David, which is called Bethlehem—because he was of the house and family of David—to register, together with Mary his espoused wife, who was with child. And it came to pass while they were there, that the days for her to be delivered were fulfilled. And she brought forth her firstborn[2] son, and wrapped him in swaddling clothes, and laid him in a manger, because there was no room for them in the inn.

And there were shepherds in the same district living in the fields and keeping watch over their flock by night. And behold, an angel of the Lord stood by them and the glory of God shone round about them, and they feared exceedingly.

And the angel said to them, "Do not be afraid, for behold, I bring you good news of great joy which shall be to all the people; for there has been born to you today in the town of David a Savior, who is Christ the Lord. And this shall be a sign to you: you will find an infant wrapped in swaddling clothes and lying in a manger." And suddenly there was with the angel a multitude of the heavenly host praising God and saying: "Glory to God in the heights and peace to the men whom He loves on earth."*[3]

And it came to pass, when the angels had departed from them into heaven, that the shepherds were saying to one another, "Let us go over to Bethlehem and see this thing that has come to pass, which the Lord has made known to us."

So they went with haste, and they found Mary and Joseph, and the babe lying in the manger. And when they had seen they understood what had been told them concerning this child. And all who heard marvelled at the things told them by the shepherds. But Mary kept in mind all these words, pondering them in her heart. And the shepherds returned, glorifying and praising God for all that they had heard and seen, even as it was spoken to them.

The Census

From the first moment of their marriage, happiness had reigned in the home of Mary and Joseph. But as they waited with tranquil joy for the coming birth of the Messias, their peace was shattered by an alarming development. Caesar Augustus, anxious to replenish the state coffers through stricter tax collection, had recently decreed that a census be taken of all the territories under Roman power. This included the country of Herod the Great, a vassal of the empire. It was left to the governor of Syria to set the date for the census in Palestine, and no doubt he had just done so at the time we are speaking of, because everyone was hastening to be enrolled (Luke 2:3). In compliance with their local customs, the people of Palestine had to go to the place of origin of their respective families instead of being registered where they then lived. It is regrettable that history has not supplied more detail about the Gospel references to the census and to the governor Cyrinus or Quirinius. This lack of information deprives us of a very valuable element for determining the exact date of Christ's birth.[4]

The decree completely disrupted the calm routine of Mary's and Joseph's life because their Davidic descent required them to leave Nazareth and go to Bethlehem to register. It meant that they had to travel more than ninety miles over winding mountain roads just when the birth of the Child was so near. Even if Mary made the journey mounted on a donkey, she must have found it very arduous.

By using the schemes of the political powers, God, from whom all authority comes, again marked the young couple with the sign of suffering. By means of these same political maneuvers and through Mary's and Joseph's obedience to the authorities, God fulfilled the prophecy (Mich. 5:1 f.) about the birth of the Messias in Bethlehem (Matt. 2:5 f.). He used the commands of the authorities and the obedience of the subjects to bring about His eternal designs.

The Birth at Bethlehem

After the difficulties of departure and the hardships of the journey itself, Mary and Joseph still had to face the task of finding somewhere to stay while they were in Bethlehem. Lodgings for rent were never plentiful in the little town, and least of all at the time of a census. There were very few large houses. Most had only one room in which space, particularly for sleeping accommodations, was at a premium (Luke 11:7). The inn, or rather the caravanserai, was simply a rectangular courtyard formed of open porches facing inward, in which people, animals, and vehicles were crowded together. Here the few places that offered even the minimum of privacy necessary for an approaching birth had already been taken. So it was through necessity rather than because of any bad will on the part of the townspeople, who were by nature most hospitable, that the young couple ultimately had to find shelter in one of the nearby caves in which the shepherds used to keep their flocks during bad weather. There Mary and Joseph found a manger, a container from which the animals ate their fodder, and they used this as a cradle for the baby. After the virginal, miraculous birth of her child, Mary laid Him in this crib with her own hands, having first wrapped Him in swaddling-clothes.

Her son was called her "firstborn" in accordance with the biblical use of the word, which gives it a juridical or legal, not a numerical meaning. Every first male child, whether or not he was eventually joined by brothers and sisters, was in principle consecrated to the exclusive service of God because he was the first male fruit of the womb and the head of his generation in the family. To be freed from exclusive service to God he had to be redeemed or bought back, and this was done for Jesus on the day of the Presentation (Luke 2:22). The firstborn son also had considerable rights in material things (cf. Exod. 13:2; 34:2). From an inscription found in the Roman catacombs we know of the case of a young Jewish woman who died giving birth to her firstborn son,[5] a cogent argument to show how erroneous it is to use the term to deny our Lady's perpetual virginity.

By allowing His own Son to be born in such circumstances, surely God wished to teach us that true happiness does not come from worldly possessions but from doing His will. Was not this to be the lesson of Christ's whole life also? Indeed, the virginal birth that had just taken place was a clear indication that this was so, as was the miraculous intervention that was to follow. God remains close to the poor who trust themselves to Him, and He shelters them under His all-powerful protection.

The Shepherds

In the fields that stretched to the east below Bethlehem, large flocks had grazed from time immemorial, destined mainly for the daily sacrifices in the Temple. Shepherds entrusted with their care, as David had been (1 Sam. 17:34f.), took turns in watching them. In practice it was impossible for these shepherds to observe the Sabbath rest and many of the ritual laws of the Jews, with the result that as a class they were despised by the Pharisees who likened them to public sinners.[6] Yet at the very moment when Christ was entering the world, it was to these very men that God spoke first, telling them the good news. These were the ones whom He wished to be the first to look upon His Incarnate Son. Once again He cast His eyes upon His humblest servants to raise them up (cf. Luke 1:48,52), and He found them eagerly receptive to the grace He offered them. During His public life, Christ was to act in the same way, revealing Himself to, and being received by, the humble and those aware of their weakness (Matt. 11:25).

The shepherds who were on watch on the night of the Nativity saw an angel. He appeared to them suddenly, and a bright light, indicative of God's presence, shone around them. The angel calmed their fear, which was similar to that felt by Zachary and Mary (Luke 1:13,30). He told them that the supernatural vision they were witnessing, far from being the sign of a chastisement to come, was instead the announcement of a great joy that would benefit all the people. In words that even the most unlettered Jews of the time could not fail to understand, he revealed to them that the Messias, the Savior (Luke 1:46,49) and Lord (Ps. 110:1) of the nation, had just been born in Bethlehem, the city of David (Luke 2:4). Conforming to biblical tradition, he gave them a sign, a verifiable proof, that his mission was as he had said (Luke 1:18 ff., 36): "You will find an infant wrapped in swaddling clothes and lying in a manger." Even at this period in Palestine, it was most unusual that a newly born child should be found in such circumstances; so when the shepherds saw the child in the manger, they would know that they had not been deceived by what they had heard in their vision. Of course, they would not be able to see the messianic character of the newly born child because no one in Israel then could even imagine that the Messias would be born in such a place. Only their faith in the angel's message would make them see beyond the outward appearances and believe that they were face to face with the expected Savior.

The moment the angel finished his message, a multitude of other angels joined him in singing the praises of God. "The army of heaven," as the Book of Kings calls the angels

(3 Kings 22:19), also had as one of their duties the praise of God (Ps. 148:2). In the present instance they used perfect parallelism to praise the happy consequences of the coming of the Messias: the external glory of God would be increased in the heights, that is, in Heaven; and peace would reign on earth among men, who had become the object of God's benevolence. This second consequence reads differently in the Latin Vulgate: peace would reign on earth among men who would give proof of good will.[7]

Mary's Thoughts

When the angels left, the shepherds talked together and decided to go and verify the truth of the message. They even went in haste, proving that they already believed it was true. They no doubt had little trouble in finding the place where the Holy Family was taking shelter, because the locality was small and they knew every corner of it. They saw at a glance the sign which the angel had given them, for they found the new-born child laid in a manger and watched over by Mary and Joseph. This was enough to convince them of the child's messianic character, so much so that they hastened to share with others what they had been *told* about Him (cf. Luke 2:17 f.). In fact, they were so enthusiastic in their description that they made those who heard them marvel. The Evangelist allows us to infer that the people to whom the shepherds spoke were the members of a group that had already assembled. Is it possible that in the interval following the Nativity, Joseph had seen fit to announce his foster-son's birth to the relatives and friends that had come with them from Nazareth for the census? We can only guess.

Mary did not forget any detail of all she heard and saw: she compared it with what she already knew, and found in it not only confirmation of her first act of faith but also a new reason for marvelling at God's loving care. Her memories of the events at the cave in Bethlehem have been preserved in the Gospels (Luke 2:19) for us, in our turn, to ponder them in our hearts. She meditated upon them, the better to learn the lessons they teach. Let us do likewise and, among other things, we shall understand with increasing clarity that God came to us through our Lady; that His transcendence is not opposed to His immanence and His loving kindness, or as St. Bernard put it: *Parvulus nimis, amabilis nimis*—His extreme humility in becoming a small child shows us how worthy of love He is; that the Incarnation should make us proud and grateful to belong to the human race, and should inspire us with respect for our own persons and those of others; that it would be most unfitting for us to exalt ourselves in the face of such great humility on God's part (Philipp. 2:3–11), or to despise anyone after seeing how privileged the poor shepherds were (Matt. 23:12; Luke 14:11; 18:14); that in the history of the Church, as at the cave in Bethlehem, we can catch enough glimpses of heaven's splendors to counteract the sight of man's wretchedness and to preserve our faith unshaken.

Ancient Traditions

The Basilica of the Nativity, which stands over the cave revered as the place of Christ's birth, holds a respected position among buildings of its kind. It was constructed in 326 at the command of Constantine the Great (306–337) and under the personal direction of St. Helena to replace a sacred grove in which the pagan worship of Adonis-Tammuz had been celebrated since 135 on the orders of the emperor Hadrian (117–138). A large part of the basilica as it now exists dates back to the period of its construction, notably the great nave with its four rows of columns. Long before the erection of the basilica, the Christians of the region venerated the cave of the Nativity. As witness to this fact we have Origen (died 254) in his book *Contra Celsum* (1, 51; Migne, *P. G.,* XI, 51): "In Bethlehem the cave in which (Jesus) was born is shown, and . . . the manger in which He was cradled. And what is thus shown is well known in these parts, even by those who are strangers to our faith." We must not forget that Origen lived in Palestine for some time. In addition, St. Justin (died 165), who came from Sichem in Samaria and was a convert from paganism, wrote in his *Dialogue with Trypho* (68, 5; Migne, *P. G.,* VI, 657) that "since Joseph had no place to stay in the village, he settled in a cave very close to Bethlehem, and it was while they were here that Mary gave birth to Christ and placed Him in a manger." The *Protoevangelium of James* also says that Christ was born in a cave (chap. 18). This evidence is very impressive, leaving little room for doubt about the authenticity of the cave in question.[8] The cave itself, under the choir of the basilica, resembles a more or less rectangular crypt about forty feet long, ten feet high, and ten feet wide.

The ancient apocryphal legend of the *Protoevangelium of James* (chap. 19) is bent on emphasizing the exceptional nature of the Savior's birth. According to it a luminous cloud, the traditional Jewish sign of God's presence among His people (cf. Exod. 40:35), filled the whole cave. Its brightness, at first unbearable, slowly decreased; and suddenly, in the midst of the divine halo, the new-born child appeared, clinging to His mother's breast. In this way the virginal nature of His birth was made clear to everyone (chap. 20).[9] As is evident, the legend does not by any means display the same delicate tact as the biblical account.

The custom of celebrating the anniversary of our Lord's

birth on December 25 existed in Rome as early as 336, and was intended to supplant the Mithraic festival in honor of the Invincible Sun (*Sol Invictus*) which was very popular in the pagan world at the time. In the East the date then observed was January 6. Actually, we lack many of the data necessary to ascertain the exact date on which we should celebrate the feast.[10]

Notes

1. At present we know only the following facts: Augustus was emperor from 30 B.C. to 14 A.D.; Saturninus was governor of Syria from 9 to 6 B.C.; Cyrinus (Quirinius) was governor of Syria from 6 to 10 A.D. The question is: had Cyrinus already been especially appointed to Syria before 6 A.D.?

2. The Evangelist uses this word with a view to the juridical effects of the birth of the first male child in a Jewish family. The term has no other implications here.

3. The Vulgate Latin translates as: "Glory to God in the highest, and on earth peace to men of good will."

4. Cf. *Dictionnaire Encyclopédique de la Bible* (Brepols, Paris, 1960), p. 1538 ff., article on "Recensement."

5. Cf. *Biblica*, 1930, pp. 373–390.

6. Cf. *Mishna*, Qidd. IV, 14; *Masses Ouvrières*, no. 188, Sept. 1962, pp. 4–17, J. Cantinat: "*L'Attitude de Jésus envers les pécheurs.*"

7. Some Greek manuscripts give "good will" in the nominative (*eudokía*) and not the genitive (*eudokías*), thus demanding the reading: "Glory to God in the heights: peace on earth: good will toward men." But this spoils the parallelism of the text and requires a conjunction to be inserted before the third phrase.

8. Cf. Vincent-Abel, *Bethléem, le sanctuaire de la Nativité* (Paris, Gabalda, 1914); DBS, article on "Bethléem"; L. H. Vincent, *L'authenticité des Lieux Saints* (Gabalda, Paris, 1932), p. 43 f.; *Revue Biblique*, 1936, p. 544 ff., "Bethléem" by L. H. Vincent.

9. Cf. *Pseudo-Matthew*, chap. 13. See also J. Hervieux, *op. cit.*, p. 56 ff.; F. Amiot, *Evangiles Apocryphes* (Paris, Fayard), 1952, p. 60 ff., 73.

10. Cf. Holzmeister, *Chronologia vitae Christi* (Rome, 1933), pp. 119–128; Dom Botte, *Les Origines de la Noël et de l'Epiphanie*, Louvain, 1932.

18

The Purification and Presentation

The Gospel Text
(Luke 2:22-35)

A<small>ND WHEN THE DAYS</small> of her purification were fulfilled according to the Law of Moses, they took him up to Jerusalem to present him to the Lord—as it is written in the law of the Lord, "Every male that opens the womb shall be called holy to the Lord"—and to offer a sacrifice according to what is said in the Law of the Lord, "a pair of turtledoves or two young pigeons."

And behold, there was in Jerusalem a man named Simeon, and this man was just and devout, looking for the consolation of Israel, and the Holy Spirit was upon him. And it had been revealed to him by the Holy Spirit that he should not see death before he had seen the Christ of the

Lord. And he came by inspiration of the Spirit into the temple. And when his parents brought in the child Jesus, to do for him according to the custom of the Law, he also received him into his arms and blessed God saying, "Now, O Lord, thou (canst) allow thy servant to go in peace, according to thy word;* because my eyes have seen thy salvation, which thou hast prepared before the face of all peoples: a light of revelation to the Gentiles, and a glory for thy people Israel."

And his father and mother were marvelling at the things spoken concerning him. And Simeon blessed them, and said to Mary his mother, "Behold, this child is destined for the fall and for the rise of many in Israel, and for a sign that shall be contradicted. And thy own soul a sword shall pierce, that the thoughts of many hearts may be revealed."

The Prescribed Ritual

When the census was over (Luke 2:1 ff.), the Holy Family left the cave and settled into a house in Bethlehem (Matt. 2:11). Apparently they had decided to reside there permanently, because they returned to Nazareth only when a whole set of extraordinary circumstances forced them to leave (Matt. 2:21 ff.). In the meantime, however, their first preoccupation was to observe the religious laws of their people. They had had the new-born child circumcised eight days after His birth and had named Him Jesus (Luke 2:21). The Law required this rite of incorporation for the male children of the Chosen People (Gen. 17:12; Lev. 12:3), and the angel Gabriel himself had announced the name to be given the child (Luke 1:31; Matt. 1:21). Now, forty days after the birth, the Holy Family set out to travel the five miles between Bethlehem and Jerusalem, on their way to the Temple for Mary's legal purification and the presentation of Jesus (Luke 2:22–24). Although the Vulgate reads "When the days of *her* purification were fulfilled" (Luke 2:22) the commonly accepted Greek text has "*their* purification." However, this is only a literary abbreviation; the two ceremonies were clearly distinct from each other, as we shall see in a moment.

Forty days after the birth of a son and eighty days after a daughter was born, every mother had to offer to the Temple a yearling lamb and a turtledove or a pigeon (Lev. 12:6)— an offering which restored her legal purity, or, in other words, allowed her once more to take her place in secular and religious society. If she was too poor to afford a lamb, she could give a second turtledove or pigeon instead (Lev. 12:8). It would be wrong to take the word "purification" here in the material sense or even in its present day moral sense. It really was nothing more than a sacred rite, older even than Israel itself and common to many races, which surrounded with respect the source of human life, namely, birth and motherhood.[1]

From the day He had struck dead the firstborn of Egypt (Exod. 12:29), God had reserved all the firstborn sons of Israel for His own service (Num. 3:13; Exod. 13:2, 13 ff.) since they were the first fruits of the womb and the future heads of families. Later, however, He accepted in their place the members of the tribe of Levi alone (Num. 3:12; 8:18), so that the firstborn of the other tribes were then freed from the sacred ministry. This freedom became effective thirty days after their birth, when they were presented to God as a sign of consecration, and five silver shekels (about seven dollars in modern currency) were paid into the Temple treasury as a sign that they had been "bought back" from the Lord.[2]

In Mary's day the requirements of both ceremonies had

become quite liberal. If the mother was suffering from fatigue or lived at a distance, she was dispensed from going to the Temple to make the offering after the forty days prescribed. In this case it was sufficient for the offering to be made at the earliest opportunity, and even then someone else could do it for her. The same held good for the presentation of the firstborn son: the important thing here was the payment of the five shekels. But Mary and Joseph did not pause to consider these alternatives, although they were well aware that they were exempt from the two prescriptions of the Law. The virginal nature of Mary's motherhood did not entail the conditions for a purification, while the fact that Christ was God's own Son did not allow of His being bought back from Him. But the society in which they lived knew nothing of all this, and the Law had not provided for any exceptions. Therefore, Mary and Joseph set out on their journey to the Temple in sheer obedience and in poverty too, for instead of a yearling lamb, they were able to give only a second turtledove (Luke 2:24).

The Canticle of Simeon

The Evangelist describes for us neither the rite of Mary's purification nor that of the presentation of Jesus, but merely indicates at the end of his account that everything prescribed in the Law was done (Luke 2:39). St. Luke had another purpose in mind, and referred to the two prescriptions of the Law merely in order to introduce the messianic revelation that they occasioned. However, the question has been asked if, in speaking of our Lord's *presentation* rather than of His being "bought back," St. Luke may not have been thinking about the sacrificial offering of the Lamb of God Himself. We cannot affirm that this was the Evangelist's thought, any more than we can say that he had in mind the gesture of Samuel's mother—leading her son to the Temple to consecrate him to the Lord's service (1 Sam. 1:24 ff.), or the prophecy of Malachias about the Lord's coming into His Temple (Mal. 3:1). Yet his silence regarding the "buying back" of Jesus does not necessarily imply a denial of it— hence the further implication that Jesus was both the Messias of Aaron (that is, of the priests in particular because, like them, He was not bought back) as well as the Messias of Israel in general.[3]

When the Holy Family reached the immense courtyard of the Temple (on their way to the Court of the Women to give their offerings to the priest on duty and to receive from him the ritual blessing) an old man stopped them, took the child in his arms for a moment, blessed God, and spoke a prophecy. This old man, about whom we know only what St. Luke tells us,[4] bore the symbolic name of Simeon, which means "God has heard." He was distinguished for his moral qualities and the ardor of his messianic hopes; he was just and pious, like Elizabeth, Zachary and Joseph, that is to say, he faithfully observed the commandments of God (Luke 1:6) and was especially diligent in carrying out the prescriptions of Jewish ritual. He awaited "the consolation of Israel," which, as Isaias said, was the coming of the Messias, God's great intervention on behalf of His Chosen People (Isa. 40:1; 49:13; 51:12; 61:2; 66:13). However, Simeon's hopes were much more specific than those of his numerous compatriots who also counted upon the deliverance of Jerusalem (Luke 2:38), for the Holy Spirit had assured him that he would not die before he had seen God's Messias (Luke 9:20; 1 Sam. 24:7; 26:9 ff.). And it was the Holy Spirit who guided him at that very moment to the Temple, led him to meet the Holy Family, made him recognize the Messias in the child they carried, and inspired the words he spoke. His words now have become the evening prayer of the church.

First, Simeon sang of the grateful joy he felt in his

heart. God was his Master, his Lord, and he, like Mary (Luke 1:37), was only His servant. But even so, God had kept His word that He would not allow him to die before showing him the Messias (Luke 2:26). Now, he said, he was ready to have the moorings broken that bound him to the shores of earth: He was prepared to allow himself to be cut loose from this world, and he could depart in peace, completely reassured about the future of Israel because with his own eyes he had seen God's salvation, the personification of the promised deliverance, Jesus the Savior-Messias (cf. Luke 1:47,69; Matt. 1:21; Isa, 40:6).

Having expressed his personal feelings, the holy old man, after the example of Isaias, unveiled the universal scope and spiritual nature of the messianic salvation that he was foretelling. God had destined and was preparing His Messias "before the face of all peoples," that is, for the sake of the whole world (cf. Isa. 19:24 f.; 42:6,10; 50:3; Gen. 13:9; 24:51).[5] The Messias was to be the light that would enlighten the pagan nations about God; He would be the truth that would deliver them from the darkness of polytheism (cf. Luke 1:79; Isa. 42:6; 49:6). This work of the Messias, the old man concluded, would shed glory on Israel, the Chosen People, because everyone would know that salvation came from the Jews, as Jesus Himself was to say later (John 4:22; Isa. 2:3 ff.; 55:4 ff.; 60:1 ff.).

The universalist tone of Simeon's canticle harmonizes very well with the context of the Third Gospel and is all the more striking here since the pagan nations are mentioned before the people of Israel. The song of the angels to the shepherds of Bethlehem had already turned attention to mankind as a whole, but it did so less precisely than Simeon's canticle; and the same holds good for the canticle of Zachary (Luke 1:79), which is in fact heavily tinged with na-

tionalism. Even the Magnificat, in speaking about the messianic glory, does not seem to go beyond the framework of
Judaism, at least if the verbs in the second part (Luke
1:50–53) are taken as referring to the past and not the future.

Israel's Unbelief

Upon hearing Simeon's words, Mary and Joseph were
astonished, or as many versions have it, they "marvelled."
In fact they must have been agreeably surprised by God's
latest intervention in addition to the previous ones; and
the old man's spontaneous knowledge of their secret gave
their faith an added foundation. Furthermore, they were
probably no less enthralled at learning more clearly the
universal extent of their son's messianic role.

But Simeon did not fall silent after he had sung his
canticle: as the Magnificat had foreseen (Luke 1:48), he
congratulated Mary and Joseph, calling down God's blessing
upon them, (Luke 2:34). Then, speaking only to Mary, he
prophesied the unbelief that her son would encounter in
many people in Israel. Contrary to the conclusions that could
be derived from his canticle, he revealed in metaphorical
form that Jesus would meet opposition as Messias, that He
would be rejected by some who would thus meet spiritual
ruin and would be believed by others who would derive
their spiritual life from their faith in Him (cf. 2 Cor.
2:14 ff.; 1 Cor. 1:2). In accordance with God's plans, He
was to be placed in men's paths as an occasion for "The fall
(or) . . . the rise of many." He was to be a sign that all
would see, to be responded to or rejected, a sign exposed to
contradiction.[6] The manner in which men would receive
Him as Messias would ultimately reveal the thoughts, the
innermost feelings, of each heart: it would be a practical
demonstration, a revelation, of each one's sincere beliefs.

This prophecy calls to mind the familiar themes of St. John's Gospel—Christ, the light that shines in the darkness, but which men do not accept because their actions are evil; the Jewish leaders discussing and, by their opposition to Him, gradually manifesting the diabolical motives that animated them (John 2:11; 3:19 ff.; 8:12 ff.; 9:38 f.; 10:30 ff., etc.). However, in St. John's Gospel, particularly in the prologue, these themes go beyond the narrow confines of the nation of Israel.

Mary's Suffering Foretold

In the middle of his prophecy about the forthcoming attitude of Israel toward the Messias, Simeon inserted a parenthetical remark. It was a thought which must have weighed on his heart, for he did not hesitate to express it at a point where it interrupted the whole rhythm of his speech. We get the impression that he could no longer keep silent about it. His words concerned our Lady directly, telling her that she would suffer by seeing her son scorned by His own people (cf. John 1:11). Her heart would be wounded, as it were: "And thy own soul a sword shall pierce."[7] In our day no one interprets this metaphor to mean that a sword of doubt pierced our Lady's heart at the Passion of her son; although some of the ancient Fathers held this view, it is a complete misinterpretation.[8]

Everything about Simeon's prophecy points to the fact that he was referring to something more than a mother's natural sharing in her son's suffering: his words to Mary break the rhythm of the passage; he spoke only to her and not to Joseph as well; he stressed her personal role in the messianic drama; his mode of address was most emphatic: "And thy own soul. . . ." Therefore he meant that God would associate the mother in an exceptional way in the pain-filled destiny of her son. Unlike the Evangelist and his readers, who are aware of the later course of events, Mary could not have known then that the metaphorical wound of which Simeon spoke would come from a real transfixion, the Passion of her son. But henceforth she would no longer be unconscious of the suffering entailed in Christ's messianic mission. From this point on, her whole life would be lived in this perspective and it would therefore be a co-operation in her son's redeeming sacrifice. The metaphor of the sword, so evocative of intense pain of soul, was sufficiently eloquent to need no explanation. The other biblical texts that use the same metaphor and that perhaps inspired Simeon to employ it (Ezech. 14:17; Isa. 53:5; Zach. 12:10), at least prove that it was a current figure of speech in Israel.

Lessons to be Learned

When we find ourselves inclined to look around for excuses to avoid doing our work, let us think about Mary's willingness to undertake the journey of ten miles to and from Jerusalem to undergo a purification which she did not need, simply because the Law, which made no provision for exceptions, demanded it. And let us also remember the divine approval she won for her obedience in the guise of Simeon's intervention. Obeying God never diminishes anyone's stature.

If we do not experience the spiritual enlightenment and consolation we so ardently desire, and if, despite the fact that we lead good, virtuous lives, we still have to bear suffering, let us think about Mary as she gradually learned her son's precise role and was promised only suffering at the very moment when she was engaged in obeying the Law of God perfectly.

With Simeon let us be assured that despite the enemy's

attacks, our Lord's coming as the Messias will always enlighten mankind for the greater glory of the new Israel, the Church.

Notes

1. Cf. P. Van Imschoot, *op. cit.*, vol. 2, p. 204 ff.; A. Clamer, *Le Lévitique* (Paris, 1939), p. 101; J. J. Weber, *op. cit.*, p. 57; P. Grelot, *Le couple humain dans l'Ecriture* (Paris, 1962), p. 31.

2. Cf. R. de Vaux, *op. cit.*, vol. 2, p. 329 ff.

3. On these different theories cf. Grelot, *op. cit.*, p. 80 f.: J. J. Weber, *op. cit.*, p. 58 f.; A. Feuillet, *op. cit.*, p. 42; R. Laurentin, *Luc I–II*, pp. 114–116.

4. There is a legend which claims to supply additional details about Simeon—that he was a great rabbi or even the High Priest, that his father was Hillel and that his son was the first Gamaliel. This legend is found in the apocryphal *Gospel of Nicodemus*, which is also called *The Acts of Pilate* (chap. XVI, 2, 6 f.; XVII, 3). See M. R. James, *The Apocrypha of the New Testament* (Oxford, 1924/55), p. 111 ff., 120.

5. See *Recherches des Sciences Religieuses*, 1928, p. 352.

6. Cf. *A la rencontre de Dieu, Mémorial Albert Gelin* (X. Mappus, Le Puy, 1961), p. 247.

7. Cf. *A la Rencontre de Dieu* (X. Mappus, Le Puy, 1961), pp. 243–263: article on "L'épreuve predite à Marie par Siméon," by A. Feuillet.

8. Cf. Migne, *P.G.*, XIII, p. 1845; XXXII, p. 964 f.; XXXIX, p. 57.

19

The Finding in the Temple

The Gospel Text
(Luke 2:41–51)

AND HIS PARENTS were wont to go every year to Jersualem
at the Feast of the Passover. And when he was twelve years
old, they went up to Jerusalem according to the custom of
the feast. And after they had fulfilled the days, when they
were returning, the boy Jesus remained in Jerusalem, and
his parents did not know it. But thinking that he was in the
caravan, they had come a day's journey before it occurred
to them to look for him among their relatives and acquaint-
ances. And not finding him, they returned to Jerusalem in
search of him.

And it came to pass after three days, that they found

him in the temple, sitting in the middle of the teachers, both listening to them and asking them questions. And all who were listening to him were amazed at his understanding and his answers. And when they saw him, they were astonished. And his mother said to him, "Son, why hast thou done so to us? Behold, thy father and I have been seeking thee sorrowing."

And he said to them, "How is it that you sought me? Did you not know that I must be about my Father's business?"[1] And they did not understand the word that he spoke to them.

And he went down with them and came to Nazareth, and was subject to them; and his mother kept all these things carefully in her heart.

The Jewish Passover in Jerusalem

The Passover first appeared as a springtime rite among nomadic or semi-nomadic shepherds, the object being to obtain fertility for the herds by sacrificing a young animal, whose blood was then smeared on the doorposts of tents or houses to ward off the forces of destruction.

The Bible changed the character of the Passover, regarding it as a rite instituted by Moses to help in freeing the Hebrews from the power of the Egyptian Pharaohs, and commanding that it be observed every year to commemorate their liberation (Exod. 12:14 ff.; Deut. 16:1 ff.).[2]

At the beginning of our era, and for many centuries before that, all male Jews of thirteen and over who lived near Jerusalem were obliged to go up to the sacred city for the celebration of the Passover, on the evening when the full moon first appeared at the end of March or the beginning of April (Exod. 23:14 ff.; Deut. 16:16; 2 Kings 23:21 ff.; Ezech. 45:21). In groups of ten they offered the blood of a lamb in the Temple, a lamb slaughtered by having its throat cut. They then roasted the lamb over a fire and ate it with bitter herbs and unleavened bread in memory of the exodus from Egypt. Women and children were free to follow the ritual or not, as they chose.

At an early date the Law of Moses made the Passover coincide with a Sabbath and followed it immediately with the feast of the Azymes, or unleavened bread, which lasted until the next Sabbath (Lev. 23:6 ff.). The feast of the Azymes was an agricultural feast marking the beginning of the grain harvest and characterized by the ritual offering of the first sheaf. The two high points of this feast were obviously the two Sabbaths between which it occurred. However, those who came to Jerusalem for the Passover but could not stay, were free to leave at the end of the first Sabbath (Luke 24:13).

The number of pilgrims who came for the Passover was enormous. The Jewish historian, Flavius Josephus, using a census taken in Nero's time as a basis, estimated that there were as many as two and a half million; but a modern author reduces this figure to 125,000.[3] They came from near and far and from every direction, grouped in caravans, singing to a musical accompaniment the gradual psalms (Ps. 120–134) that express the joy of approaching the House of God. Upon arriving, they camped all around the city, but especially on the western slope of Mount Olivet from which they were able to see into the courtyard of the Temple and could follow the ceremonies in detail. Many of them stayed until the end of the feast of the Azymes, eight days later, taking advantage of the unaccustomed leisure to make up their arrears in ritual obligations and to listen to the rabbis lecturing on religion in the porches, courtyards, and outer parts of the Temple.

The Holy Family's Pilgrimage

The Holy Family never omitted the paschal pilgrimage (Luke 2:41) despite the fact that they had long been re-settled in Nazareth (Luke 2:39; Matt. 2:23), far from the capital and its Temple. Joseph did not even stop to con-sider that the distance could dispense him from the pil-grimage, to which incidentally, he alone of the family was bound. Even more, he used to bring Jesus and Mary with him. On the occasion to which the Gospel refers, he had an additional reason for bringing his foster-son, who was now twelve years old and would soon cease to be a child in the eyes of the religious Law: soon He would become "a son of the precept," a *bar mitsvah*, subject to the precepts of the Law. Accordingly, it was fitting that He should become ac-customed to this new way of life.

Everything went well until the time came to return home, "after they had fulfilled the days" (Luke 2:43), that is, at the end of the week of the Azymes, eight days after their arrival. On the morning of departure all the caravans that had come from distant places set out from the city in a great dis-array of people, animals and vehicles, spread out along the roads in endless lines. The members of each caravan had agreed beforehand to meet at a certain stopping place along the route on the evening of the first day to allow families to regroup and to restore the order of march (Luke 2:44). Counting on the confusion of departure, Jesus had deliber-ately withdrawn from His relatives' vigilance in order to remain in Jerusalem. His reply when He was found again leaves no doubt on this subject. But Mary and Joseph did not suspect for a moment that this could be the case. Until the evening of the first day of travelling they thought He was with a group of their relatives or friends, as is clear from the fact that they first looked for Him there when they found that He was missing (Luke 2:44). Their anxiety, about which Mary was to speak later (Luke 2:48), must not have become really acute until the next morning when the caravan had been fully re-organized and they were forced to admit that Jesus had not joined any of the groups that composed it.

Finding Jesus: His Reply

Retracing their steps, they enquired about their Son among the groups of stragglers they met along the way. In Jerusalem itself they searched all the places where Jesus was likely to be, but in vain. It was only on the following day, the third day of separation, that they finally discovered Him in one of the outer parts of the Temple, seated in the middle of a group of teachers of religion. They were greatly surprised at the serenity He displayed while listening to and interrogating the teachers, who were no doubt discussing some point of the Law of Moses (cf. John 5:39). The boy was perfectly at ease, and apparently untroubled by having lost contact with His family; for His close attention to the discussion, His questions, and His answers made all His hearers marvel.

When Mary saw this, she must have realized that Jesus had deliberately remained there. Since she knew that her Son was the Messias (Luke 1:31f., 43f.; 2:11ff., 29ff.), perhaps she thought that He had already in some way begun the mission which He had been given. As soon as she could speak to Him without causing undue comment, she asked Him: "Son, why hast thou done so to us? Behold, thy father and I have been seeking thee sorrowing." Her words reveal what was in her heart—her motherly love, for she questioned Jesus as her *son*; her delicate tact, for she mentioned Joseph's anxiety before her own; her keen sensibility, for she had received a most painful shock at the thought that she might have lost her beloved child; her astonishment at the mystery in which she found herself involved.

As He habitually did later, often with the idea of riveting His listeners' attention, Jesus now gave His answer in the form of a question: "How is it that you sought me? Did you not know that I must be about my Father's business?" As we have noted, the Greek turn of phrase in the second question here can also be translated: "Did you not know that I must be in my Father's *house?*" In the opinion of many authors, this version would fit better with Mary's question, for it would mean in effect: "You should have known where to find me, for I could be nowhere else but in my Father's house, the Temple."[4] But the first translation, which we have kept and which is quite generally adopted, does not lack biblical foundations (cf. 1 Cor. 7:33; 1 Tim. 4:15) and gives one of the most acceptable meanings. According to this version, Jesus meant: "Did you not know that my Father's business is more important than yours?" The most striking part of His answer, however, is not precisely this but rather His use of the two words "must" and "Father." He stated that He had remained in Jerusalem because He *had to (dei)* be there, and in addition He called God His *Father*, contrasting Him with His earthly, legal father, whom Mary had just mentioned. Thus He emphasized His *obligation* to act as He did, and at the same time He revealed the source of that obligation—the will of God, His heavenly Father. During His public life, He would unceasingly invoke God's will as the basis for His actions, His teaching and even His very death (Matt. 16:21; 24:6; Luke 9:22; 17:25; 21:9; 24, 26). His food would be to do the will of Him who sent Him (John 4:34; 6:39 f.; Luke 22:42), the will of Him who could command Him directly and without regard for

His human aversion to pain and sorrow. This was the case in the Agony in the Garden, and also in His ties with those He loved, even His own family. Was He not to say later: "Whoever does the will of God, he is my brother and sister and mother" (Mark 3:35)? Thanks to the revelations of His public life, we can understand more clearly His reply to His mother. He showed that in His human nature He was conscious of the mystery of His Divine Person, for He spoke of His Father in a unique sense, allowing us a glimpse of His transcendence. He attributed to Himself very special duties in regard to the Father and claimed absolute independence in the fulfillment of these duties. For Him, God's own Son, the divine will was sovereign and took precedence over the tenderest earthly affections. But to interpret His answer properly we would have to recapture His intonation as He spoke, for His great love for Mary and Joseph must assuredly have been evident in His voice and manner.

Mary's Incomprehension

The Evangelist tells us that Mary and Joseph did not understand their son's reply, but he does not specify exactly what they did not comprehend. Was it the transcendence which Jesus attributed to Himself? Many authors think it was. Or was it, as some say, the absolute independence that He claimed? Or did His parents rather not understand the sudden and unexpected way in which He dropped His claim to independence, for the Gospel in fact seems to imply that they were surprised to see Him once more *subject* to them. Many authors hold that this was the case, and they even regard the Evangelist's final remark as confirmation of their theory: "And his mother kept all these things carefully in her heart" (Luke 2:51).

At any rate, this text compels us to admit that, in a sense,

Mary had to advance in faith. The mystery of her son was fully revealed to her only as events unfolded. The finding in the Temple also shows us the beginning of the fulfillment of Simeon's prophecy. Here, suffering in the form of anxiety pierced Mary's heart and was multiplied by her increased uncertainty about the future—a foretaste of the suffering she would feel on Calvary and during the three days' burial in the tomb.

Practical Conclusions

Let us, too, give way to God's will when required to do so. If we are parents, let us realize that our children belong first to God, and let us not run counter to His ownership, especially when it is a question of a vocation. Let us not indulge in self-pity when we do not fully understand God's plans for us or for those we love—our children, for example. Let us remember that God is simply treating us as He once treated His own Mother. If we have the misfortune to lose Jesus through our own fault, not against our will as Mary lost Him, let us follow her example and make haste to find Him again by searching for Him, especially in His Father's house.

Notes

1. In the Greek there is no noun expressed—"the (things) of my Father." This leaves a certain vagueness and allows many authors to translate it as "the *house* of my Father"; "my Father's house."
2. Cf. R. de Vaux, *op. cit.*, vol. 2 (Paris, 1960), p. 383 ff.
3. Flavius Josephus, *Jewish War*, VI, 9, 3; Philo, *De Monarchia*, II, 1; J. Jeremias, *Jerusalem zur Zeit Jesu*, vol. 1, p. 96.
4. See the commentaries of Plummer, Lagrange, Valensin-Huby, Marchal, Creed, Balmforth, and others.

20

The Wedding Feast at Cana

The Gospel Text
(John 2:1-11)

Aᴺᴰ ᴏɴ ᴛʜᴇ ᴛʜɪʀᴅ ᴅᴀʏ a wedding took place at Cana of
Galilee,¹ and the mother of Jesus was there. Now Jesus too
was invited to the marriage, and also his disciples. And the
wine having run short,² the mother of Jesus said to him,
"They have no wine." And Jesus said to her, "What dost
thou want of me, woman?* My hour has not yet come."
His mother said to the attendants, "Do whatever he tells
you."

Now six stone water-jars were placed there, after the
Jewish manner of purification,³ each holding two or three
measures.⁴ Jesus said to them, "Fill the jars with water."

And they filled them to the brim. And Jesus said to them, "Draw out now, and take to the chief steward." And they took it to him.

Now when the chief steward had tasted the water after it had become wine, not knowing whence it was (though the attendants who had drawn the water knew), the chief steward called the bridegroom, and said to him, "Every man at first sets forth the good wine, and when they have drunk freely, then that which is poorer. But thou hast kept the good wine until now."

This first of his signs Jesus worked at Cana of Galilee; and he manifested his glory, and his disciples believed in him.

The Invitation to the Wedding

More than twenty years had elapsed between the finding in the Temple and the wedding at Cana. For Jesus, who was now over thirty (Luke 3:23), they had been the long, obscure years of His life in Nazareth, among His relatives and in His carpenter's shop (Mark 6:3). Two months before the wedding, He had decided to leave His life of obscurity and take the first steps toward His public ministry near Jericho in the valley of the Jordan—His meeting with the Precursor, John the Baptist; His baptism with water; His victory over the devil in the desert; the choice of His first disciples (Mark 1:9 ff.; Matt. 3:13 ff.; Luke 3:21 ff.; John 1:29 ff.).

It was just after He had returned from this journey that He went to Cana for the wedding of a relative or friend. According to most authors, "the third day" mentioned by St. Luke is a piece of chronological information, more or less closely connected with our Lord's decision to leave the banks of the Jordan and return to Galilee. Other authors, however, believe that mention of the third day has only a symbolic significance: "this first of his signs" at Cana, manifesting "his glory" (John 2:11), announced the "hour" (John 2:4) of His supreme glorification by His death and His resurrection on the third day.[5]

The distance between Nazareth and Cana is little more than four miles. Jesus came accompanied by His Mother and His disciples, who had also been invited. One of these disciples, Nathanael, was from Cana (John 21:2), and many authors have thought that the invitation came from him; but actually there were so many other good reasons for the invitation that none can be singled out with certainty. In a sense, Jesus was going to spend His last peaceful days in the place where He had grown up. The Passover was close at hand, with its obligatory pilgrimage to the Temple in Jerusalem; and this Passover, soon to be followed by His long ministry on the shores of the Sea of Galilee, would really inaugurate His preaching of the Kingdom.

The Bible has not preserved for us a detailed description of the ancient marriage ceremonies of Israel: yet here and there it does contain sufficient allusions to them to allow us to discern the essentials. We have already spoken about this matter in connection with our Lady's wedding, but perhaps a brief review of the ceremony will not be out of place here. Accompanied by friends and musicians, the bridegroom went to the home of his bride, where he found her veiled and waiting, surrounded by girls, and ready to follow him. Then, to the sound of love songs extolling the newlyweds' good qualities, he led her to his own house, where a great feast had been prepared, to which many guests had been invited. At the feast itself, however, the men and women did not mingle but formed two separate groups. Because the wedding feast was usually followed by several others, supplies were carefully gathered over a long period beforehand; but it could sometimes happen that, for a variety of reasons, they would not be sufficient to meet the demand.

Water Changed into Wine

At the wedding in Cana, it was the supply of wine that ran out before the feast was over. But none of the men even suspected it, as is evident from the chief steward's remark when he had tasted the miraculous wine. Praising what he regarded as the bridegroom's thoughtful foresight, he exclaimed: "Every man at first sets forth the good wine, and when they have drunk freely, then that which is poorer. But thou hast kept the good wine until now" (John 2:10).[6]

Only the women were aware of the threatened shortage, no doubt because they were in closer contact with those serving the guests and were themselves involved to some degree in the catering. Mary, who was of course among the women there, rose from her place and, before it would be too late, went and whispered to her son the simple words: "They have no wine." Obviously she was counting on Him to take care of everything.[7] Her actions here, while analogous to those of Lazarus's sisters (John 11:3), at the same time reveal her confidence and her tender compassion. At first glance, however, the answer she received seems anything but favorable. "What dost thou want of me, woman?" Jesus said to her, "My hour has not yet come." This reply, which, as we shall soon see, has always taxed the wisdom of scripture scholars, did not deter her. Her feminine, motherly intuition assured her that she should remain confident. Counting on her son's intervention in some way as yet unknown to her, she hastened back to those who were serving and alerted them, telling them to follow the directions that her son would give them: "Do whatever he tells you" (cf. Gen. 41:55).

And our Lord actually did intervene quickly. First, He ordered the six stone jars that stood at the entrance to be filled with water. These receptacles were normally meant to hold water for the numerous ritual ablutions that were customary among the Jews. The Gospels tell us about the ritual washing of cups, pitchers, bronze dishes, of hands and even of feet (Mark 7:3 f.; Matt. 23:35; Luke 7:44; 9:38 f.). The total amount contained in the six jars was at least 120 gallons since each held two or three measures, a measure being equivalent to about ten gallons. No doubt the requirements of the wedding feast explain the presence of so many large containers. There was only one fountain and that was relatively far away and on a lower level; so that it was quite a task to replenish the supply. The Evangelist also observes that the attendants knew very well where the miraculous wine came from (John 2:9).

When the jars had been filled to the brim (John 2:7), our Lord told the attendants to take some to the chief steward, whose duty it was to determine the amount of water to be mixed with each type of wine. It was at this point that the water was changed into wine of an exceptionally good quality.

The Disciples' Faith and Ours

It is probable that the miracle did not become known to all until the feast had ended and the guests were departing. When the disciples learned of it, they experienced an increase in their new-found faith. They were more certain that he was the Messias (cf. John 1:41 ff.), as the Evangelist points out: "He manifested his glory, and his disciples believed in Him" (John 2:11). "In the language of the New Testament, the glory of God is . . . the divine power that multiplies miracles, thus manifesting God's presence."[8] In working the miracle, Jesus had directly willed this result. This much is obvious from His previous declaration to Nathanael: "Because I said to thee that I saw thee under the fig tree, thou dost believe. Greater things than these shalt thou see" (John 1:50 f.). "The water changed into wine was not only a miracle: it was also a *sign* (as the Evangelist says). A sign can have a certain value in itself, but it really receives its full meaning only from that to which it refers (namely, Christ's glory)."⁹

Unlike the first disciples, we have been educated by the whole of revelation; so we understand better than they the spiritual riches contained in the miraculous sign at Cana. The mere recollection of these riches serves to re-animate our faith. But we shall confine ourselves here to recalling the principal ones—God's great condescension in taking care of our smallest needs; His creative power, making child's play of difficulties and showing us that transubstantiation presents no problem to Him; the sacred character of marriage, as shown by Christ's presence at the feast; the great value of filial respect, already pointed out in the Decalogue (Exod. 20:12); Mary's quick compassion for even our smallest troubles; her incomparable power of intercession with her son and her practical association with the distribution of God's graces.

In addition to the first sign at Cana, we have seen many other signs of Christ's glory, especially those of the Resurrection and the Ascension; so with St. John we believe that His glory is that of "the only-begotten of the Father" (John 1:14). The signs reported by the Evangelists, by St. John in particular, prove to us that "Jesus is the Christ, the Son of God" (John 20:31).

Christ's Reply to Mary

Our Lord's reply to His mother at the wedding feast at Cana has been interpreted in very many different ways, so many in fact that it would be impossible to describe them all. Indeed, it would take us too long even to enumerate them; and so, we shall simply outline just a few.

Following St. Augustine and St. Thomas,[10] many commentators hold, with various slight differences, that when our Lord was confronted with His mother's explicit request for a miracle, He refused to perform it, expressing His refusal in such terms as to emphasize His desire to withdraw His work and His messianic mission from all human influence, even that of His mother. Now, as He had done at the finding in the Temple (Luke 2:49), He proclaimed that He was looking to His heavenly Father alone and to the "hour" fixed by Him. That was why He called His mother "woman," a title that stressed His emancipation from her parental influence. Hence He meant: "What have we in common as regards my mission? The hour which my Father has appointed for me to manifest myself by miracles has not yet come!" Yet, having laid down this principle, our Lord did perform the miracle, either out of consideration for His mother or for some other reason. And because Mary had an intuition that this would happen, she told the servants to do as her son said.

This opinion is based on the fact that in the Old Testament, the words which Christ used ("What dost thou want of me?") sometimes have the meaning of refusal or lack of communication. Literally they mean, "What (is this) to thee and to me?" (cf. Os. 14:9; 2 Kings 3:13; Jos. 22:24). The opinion which we have just outlined is also based upon the word "woman" and upon the fact that in the end our Lord did perform the miracle which Mary requested.

While accepting this theory in its essentials, some authors believe that the "hour" of which Christ spoke was that of His Passion and death. During His public ministry, they say, He would not listen to any requests from His mother, but when the hour of His Passion and death arrived, then she could ask of Him whatever she wanted.[11] Therefore, by His reply, our Lord was telling her about His new state and was promising her that, later, He and she would be even more closely united than before. Again, from Cana to the Passion, Mary appears in the Gospels in a passive role only. The authors who give this meaning to the word "hour" base their conclusion on several other passages in St. John's Gospel (John 7:30; 8:20; 13:1; 17:1).

Nowadays there is a tendency to regard our Lord's "hour" as His final glorification, which was inaugurated by His redeeming death.[12] The whole incident then would be understood in this light. Thus Mary simply stated the embarrassing plight of the wedding party: "They have no wine." But our Lord in His reply took His stand on a higher plane, speaking from the point of view of a transcendent universe, different from that of even the holiest of men, and looking at everything in the light of the mission He had received from His Father. Having in mind the biblical literary device of using wine as an image of the benefits that accrue from the messianic alliance, He interpreted His mother's plea as a request for that messianic "wine," and so He replied that it was premature: "You are asking for something that I have no intention of giving now. My hour has not yet come, the hour of the redeeming cross, when the Church, the source of the messianic benefits (that is, the sacraments, and the Wine of the Eucharist), shall be definitively founded." But He was not in any way reprimanding her, for He could scarcely have reproached her for not knowing the secrets of God's plan. He was simply speaking to her enigmatically, thereby putting her faith to the test. And indeed Mary was so far from feeling repulsed that she said to the servants: "Do whatever he tells you." Just as at the finding in the Temple, she did not understand; yet she had confidence, and our Lord worked the miracle.[13]

The principal difficulty in the Gospel account is that it shows Christ granting His mother's request after apparently repulsing her. A recent suggestion is that we should regard the second part of His reply as a question: "Has not my hour come yet?" Other New Testament texts favor this interrogative sense (Mark 8:17; Luke 23:39; John 18:11); moreover, it was formerly accepted by several Greek Fathers. The rest of the passage would then be as follows. Mary showed her concern about the lack of wine without adverting to her son's power to remove the difficulty. He reproached her for thinking differently from Him at that moment, for being pre-occupied with material worries, and for forgetting both His power as Messias and His mission, which was beginning. It was as if He said: "Don't you know, then, that the hour has come for me to show myself as the Messias and therefore to work miracles?" Mary understood His affectionate reproach and consequently told the servants to obey her son. His reproval here, like the one at the finding in the Temple (Luke 2:49), was not aimed at any lack of faith on Mary's part, but rather at her slowness, as it were, in understanding the messianic mystery.[14]

It is true that the texts from St. John's Gospel in which the word "hour" refers to our Lord's definitive glorification (John 7:30; 8:20) may be quoted against this interpretation. But the answer to this objection is that Christ's miracles were actually the beginning of this final "hour."[15]

We regret that we cannot mention here any more of the theories suggested; many of them are quite different from the others, are very ingenious, and contain some excellent points.[16] However, those that we have discussed are more than enough to show, by their very differences, how far we still are, unfortunately, from holding the key to our Lord's reply to His mother at the wedding feast at Cana.

Notes

1. There was another Cana, Cana of Aser, which lay in the direction of Tyre.
2. Some manuscripts have: "They had no wine because the wedding wine was all gone."
3. Ritual washing of hands (Mark 7:3 f), of feet (Luke 7:44), and of cups and dishes (Matt. 23:25).
4. A measure was approximately ten gallons.
5. C. H. Dodd, *The Interpretation of the Fourth Gospel* (Cambridge, 1953), p. 230; M. E. Boismard, *Du Baptême à Cana* (Paris, 1956), p. 15, 136; J. P. Charlier, *Le Signe de Cana* (Brussels, 1959), p. 45 ff.; H. Troadec, *Le Message de Saint Jean* (Paris, 1962), p. 30. Besides, there are many differences of opinion between these authors: see also Max Thurian, *Marie, Mère du Seigneur, Figure de l'Eglise* (Taizé, 1962), p. 180 ff.
6. It is hard to reconcile this remark with the meaning sometimes given to verse 3 (cf. J. P. Charlier, *op. cit.*, p. 46).
7. Cf. A. George, *Jésus, notre vie* (Paris, 1958/61), p. 29; H. Troadec, *op. cit.*, p. 31; M. E. Boismard, *op. cit.*, p. 143 f.
8. M. E. Boismard, *Le Prologue de Saint Jean* (Paris, 1953), p. 71.
9. J. P. Charlier, *op. cit.*, p. 58.
10. St. Augustine, *In Joannis Evangelium tractatus*, VIII; Migne, P.L. 35, 1455, 9; St. Thomas, *In Evangelium B. Joannis expositio* (Turin, 1919), p. 79.
11. F. M. Braun, *La Mère des Fidèles* (Paris-Tournai, 1953/54), p. 47 ff.; P. Gächter, *op. cit.*, p. 155 ff.
12. Cf. A. Feuillet, *Etudes Johanniques* (1962), p. 13 ff.
13. Cf. A. Feuillet, *op. cit.*, p. 25 ff.; *Maria*, vol. 6, p. 52 f.
14. Cf. M. E. Boismard, *Du Baptême à Cana*, p. 149 ff.
15. Cf. M. E. Boismard, *op. cit.*, p. 154.
16. Cf. H. Van den Bussche, *L'Evangile du Verbe*, vol. 1 (Brussels, 1959), p. 37 ff.; J. P. Charlier, *Le Signe de Cana*, p. 52 ff. See also *Maria*, vol. 6, p. 53, note 88, p. 68; M. E. Boismard, *op. cit.*, p. 133 ff.

21

During Our Lord's Public Life

The Silence of the Gospels

THE GOSPELS are very sparing with information about Mary during our Lord's public life, reporting none of her words and saying nothing about her married life or where she lived. The result is that we are forced to speculate about the date of Joseph's death and to wonder whether our Lady remained in Nazareth or placed herself at her son's service along with a group of holy women. Indeed, we can do little more than devise theories about these important points. It is conceivable that Mary may have followed Jesus as He moved from place to place, if she was then a widow, if some of her women relatives (Salome, for instance) were already among her Son's followers, or if her Son, whose heart was touched by the plight of parents in distress, did not wait until He was dying on the cross to have pity on His own mother's loneliness. But it is equally conceivable that even if she was a widow, our Lord deliberately left her in Nazareth to show more clearly that He was free from all human influence in His mission. If that was the case, however, it is harder to explain why the description of one of His preaching visits to Nazareth seems to imply that only His female cousins ("sisters") still lived there (Mark 6:3: "And are not also his sisters here with us?").

For this important period in Mary's life, the Gospels supply us with only two or three pieces of indirect information, and we shall see that even these are not as clear as we should like.

Passovers Spent with Jesus

After the wedding feast at Cana, our Lord traveled the nineteen miles to Capharnaum, a small frontier town in Galilee situated on the northern shore of the Lake of Genesareth (John 2:12). Soon He would make this town the center of His preaching, but now He remained there only a few days. He was accompanied by the same group that had been with Him at Cana, namely, His mother and His disciples. It was here that the disciples received the title of "brethren," as they were called in the primitive Church (Acts 1:15). The Jewish Passover was drawing near, and He was going to go down to Jerusalem to observe it there (John 2:13). But He no doubt went first to Capharnaum, which was even farther from Jerusalem than Cana, in order to give His disciples, who were natives of the region, a chance to rejoin their families, and to organize with them the caravan in which they would all travel to the capital for the Passover. This explains Mary's presence, too, for she also was going on the pilgrimage to Jerusalem, as she did every year (Luke 2:41).[1]

It is not impossible that, two years later and under similar conditions, our Lady was associated with her Son's last Passover pilgrimage, for we know that she was present at the foot of the cross with the group of holy women who had followed our Savior from Galilee (John 19:25; Matt. 27:55).

Family Reactions

From the beginning of His missionary activity in Capharnaum, our Lord was much sought after. The people thronged around Him, even invading His dwelling-place and giving Him no time to eat. But His relatives were worried by the stir He was creating: they did not yet believe in the authenticity of His mission (John 7:5) and, as a result of malicious rumors, they were inclined to conclude that He was acting irrationally. Accordingly, they wanted to seize Him and make Him return to His former way of life (Mark 3:20 f.). Mary was in this group of relatives, not because she thought as they did—we are assured of her faith in her son (Luke 1:45; John 2:3 f.)—but no doubt because she had been forced to accompany them in order to ensure the success of their scheme. However, her own personal intention must have been to exercise a restraining influence on the others.

When His relatives arrived and asked to speak to Him, our Lord was in the middle of a crowd seated about Him and listening attentively. Taking advantage of the situation, He used it to teach His audience that there are ties greater than those of blood: "Whoever does the will of God, he is my brother and sister and mother" (Mark 3:35). In this way

He began His teaching about the spiritual kingdom, and He did so in such a striking manner because He well knew His listeners' worldly and nationalistic aspirations (cf. Matt. 20:20 ff.). He spoke in almost paradoxical terms and used the setting to enforce His point by first asking a question, then looking around at His audience, and finally extending His arm as He supplied the answer (Mark 3:31 ff.). His intention was not by any means to repudiate the bonds of blood relationship. Instead, He would soon take pains to recall forcefully God's decree in this regard (Mark 7:10) and would often make plain His respect for family ties, notably in the episode of the widow of Naim.

This, too, is the sense in which we should understand His well-known declaration about the necessity of *hating* one's family in order to be His disciple. Here He was using a Hebrew idiom ("to hate" meaning "to love less"), and simply wished to say that where there is a conflict between our family's wishes and God's will, we should do what God wants (Luke 14:26). The light which He was to shed on the divine will would reveal to many people a source of frequent conflict, of which they were hitherto unaware, and would consequently cause dissension in many families: "Do not think that I came to send peace upon the earth. I have come to bring a sword, not peace . . . , and a man's enemies will be those of his own household" (Matt. 10:34 ff.).

Praise of Mary

The Gospel also tells us indirectly of the praise which our Lord bestowed on His mother. A woman, filled with admiration for Him, cried out: "Blessed is the womb that bore thee, and the breasts that nursed thee." He replied: "Rather, blessed are they who hear the word of God and keep it" (Luke 11:27). His answer was designed to correct an outlook that was confined to the things of the flesh. Of course He did not deny the value of such things; otherwise He would not have used the word "Rather. . . ." Instead, He wished to raise His listeners above the material level to that of the spirit. In short, His answer to the woman meant that Mary's greatness depended less on the material fact of her motherhood than upon the dispositions of soul which went with it—her faith and perfect conformity to the will of God—precisely those things which Elizabeth was inspired by God to praise in her (Luke 1:45). The paradoxical tone of our Lord's answer was designed to bring home this doctrine more forcefully. So it should not obscure His admiration for His mother, who unceasingly lived in accordance with this teaching.

Note

1. For a different interpretation of John 2:12, see *Mélanges A. Robert*, p. 411 ff.: "Le premier séjour de Jésus à Capharnaum," by D. Buzy.

22

During the Passion

Before Our Lord's Trial

Sᴉɴᴄᴇ Mᴀʀʏ was present on Calvary, it follows that she had come to Jerusalem for the Passover, which began officially on Good Friday evening. That much is certain; but we can only guess about how and when she arrived in the holy city.

It is possible that she stayed in Galilee during our Lord's ministry in Judea and simply joined the usual group of pilgrims from Nazareth or Capharnaum. Or, instead of going through Samaria, she might have travelled with her fellow-pilgrims by way of Jericho and found Jesus there, preparing to go up to the capital Himself (Mark 10:46). If this is what happened, then she was present at all the events of Holy Week. But it is also possible that, even though she did go by way of Jericho, she did not find Jesus there because He had already left, and that she did not meet Him until some time later in Holy Week. Finally, it is possible that she followed her Son throughout the period of His ministry in Judea and was therefore with Him on His last pilgrimage, living among the group of holy women from Galilee who were later to keep her company on Calvary.

On the Road to Calvary

Whichever of these theories we may adopt, we know that Mary was able to follow at least the last scenes of the Passion; the pilgrims, especially those who came from afar, arrived in Jerusalem on the eve of the Passover at the latest so as to have time to make camp near the city and get some rest.

In any case, it is inconceivable that Mary was in the garden of the Agony before her Son's arrest, that she was able to gain entry to the High Priest's house with St. Peter, or that she was present at the public events of our Lord's trial before Pilate. The circumstances were such that it was scarcely possible for her to have witnessed any of these occurrences. On the other hand, it would be very surprising if she had not been waiting to see her son at some point along the road from the pretorium to Calvary, like the holy women of Jerusalem. It is very probable that this meeting between mother and son, now commemorated in the fourth Station of the Cross, did occur; and we can perhaps see a reference to it in the texts of the first three Gospels which refer to the group of friends and holy women that were watching from a distance on Calvary (Matt. 27:55 f.; Mark 15:40 f.; Luke 23:49). In fact this is the same group that St. John later describes as being near the cross when Christ uttered His second or third words (John 19:25 f.), when some of the crowd had dispersed.

We can easily imagine the suffering and mutual compassion, the courageous acceptance and the love in the glances exchanged between mother and son. What a comfort it must have been for our Lord's human nature to feel the presence of a heart such as His mother's, perfectly in harmony with His own!

On Calvary

As soon as she was able, Mary drew close to her crucified son. She met with no opposition from the soldiers; four of them, commanded by a centurion, had been left simply to ensure that the sentence of death was carried out in full (Matt. 27:36).

Our Lady was accompanied by several Galilean women who, a long time before, had placed themselves at Christ's service—Mary Magdalene; Mary, the wife of Cleophas; and our Lady's "sister," Mary. We do not know if the word "sister" here simply means cousin and refers to Salome, St. John's mother. The probability that our Lady and Salome were related would explain why Christ confided His mother to St. John, who would then be His cousin. In addition to the well-beloved disciple, Mary had with her all her son's friends (Luke 23:49), especially Nicodemus and Joseph of Arimathea, who would soon take steps to ensure the burial of Christ.

Despite the unimaginable pain she felt as she witnessed her son's death on the cross, Mary accepted her own sufferings with the same dispositions and the same intentions as Christ accepted His (Luke 2:35). Thus, before St. Paul put the doctrine into words, she "filled up in (her) flesh . . . what (was) lacking (providentially and in the sphere of application) of the sufferings of Christ . . . for . . . the Church" (Col. 1:24). Here, on Calvary, she was truly the Mother of Sorrows, honored in our liturgy and invoked by

Jacopone da Todi in the thirteenth century in his *Stabat Mater dolorosa.*

It is useless to try to imagine exactly our Lady's bearing as Jesus hung on the cross. Suffice it to say that the Greek word, which is usually translated as "standing" near the cross ("Now there were standing by the cross of Jesus his mother. . . ." [John 19:25]), simply implies our Lady's presence on Calvary and is not intended to describe her precise posture there.

Christ's Last Words to His Mother

Far from being preoccupied with His own sufferings, Jesus was concerned about the pain that others, particularly His mother, were enduring. Despite His agony, He wished to procure for her, in the person of His beloved disciple, the support that she would need. "Woman, behold thy son," He said to her, designating St. John. And to John He added, "Behold thy mother" (John 19:25 f.).

As St. Ambrose says, these words were Christ's "family testament." That is true; but they are also confirmation of Mary's universal spiritual motherhood, which is based upon the very fact of the Incarnation, as Pius XII recalled in his encyclical on the Mystical Body. Modern authors, following Origen, readily point out the frequency with which the characters in St. John's Gospel represent whole categories of people. Even the beloved disciple, St. John, is himself an image of all the Christians whom God loves because they keep His commandments. Hence in him all those good Christians who have become Christ's brothers have been given Mary as their Mother. Mary is then the new Eve, the ideal woman, Mother of the new Israel, the Church, through which God prolongs on earth the saving action of His Son and through which He deals with men like a mother: "As one whom the mother caresseth," said Yahweh, "so will I comfort you" (Isa. 66:13).

With St. John, let us esteem at its true value the honor of having such a mother. Just as "the (beloved) disciple took her into his home" (John 19:27), let us, too, receive her into ours. St. John became her pupil to obtain a more sublime knowledge of the Word Incarnate: let us also listen to her, and we shall come to know Christ ever better.

23

The Infant Church

The Resurrection

O N THE EVENING of Good Friday, before the Sabbath rest began at sunset, the holy women sat in front of the sepulcher, attentively following the actions of Nicodemus and Joseph of Arimathea, who were engaged in putting Christ's body in the tomb. The women took particular note of the way the two disciples placed their Lord's body in the burial chamber. They intended to come back on the morning after the Sabbath rest to express their personal love for Jesus. They would add their own gifts of burial spices to Nicodemus's princely offering (seventy pounds of myrrh and aloes), a practice permitted by custom in Palestine during the three days after death. So, at sunrise on Easter Sunday morning, the women set out for the tomb, anxious about finding some passers-by to roll back the heavy stone that sealed the entrance. Their whole attitude proves that they did not even dream that they would find a risen Christ. They expected to see only a dead body: many startling surprises awaited them (Mark 15:46 ff.; 16:1 ff.).

Although Mary had been present on Calvary, she was not in the group that set out to render final homage to her Son's lifeless body. Her absence is striking, and many authors, apparently with good reason, see in it a proof that the risen Lord had already shown Himself to her in the early hours of the morning, with the result that she saw no purpose in going to the tomb, as she would otherwise have been bound to do. It is not hard to see how very fitting it would be for our Lord to have appeared to our Lady first. For instance, how could He, the model of filial love and respect, have forsaken His Mother who was so filled with faith, while He went to appear to His disciples, who had either fled, or denied Him, or returned home in despair? Perhaps the reason why the Gospel does not mention this first apparition is a mother's testimony on her son's behalf was not acceptable in law; and perhaps there were other reasons unknown to us.

Mary at Pentecost

From the Ascension until Pentecost our Lady lived in the Cenacle in Jerusalem with the Apostles, the holy women, and her relatives who had finally rallied to her son's cause (Acts 1:12–14). She joined in the community's prayer for the coming of the Holy Spirit who had been promised, and in this way she prepared for the birth of the Church. As we remember, her prayer at the wedding feast at Cana had been most effective; and now she who had been present at the beginning of the Gospel was to be present also at the beginning of the Church.

For St. Luke, author of the third Gospel and the Acts

of the Apostles, Mary's presence in the Cenacle had perhaps a very special significance, that of a unique preparation for the outpouring of the Spirit upon the infant Church. At the beginning of his Gospel St. Luke speaks about the descent of the Holy Spirit on Mary at the Annunciation and about Elizabeth's joy at the Visitation (Luke 1:35,41), while at the beginning of the Acts he relates the descent of the Spirit upon the Apostles at Pentecost and its happy results (Acts 2:1 ff.). It seems therefore that the Evangelist meant to establish an analogy between the two series of events, and that he regarded the first as the prelude to the second. Christ's virginal birth then appears "as the first eschatological outpouring of the Spirit upon the world . . . , the (beginning) of the new creation" (J. Schmitt), and Mary herself, in her all-important role, appears as the instrument and, in a sense, as the very type or figure of final salvation. Therefore, her presence and her actions in the Cenacle would have particular importance.[1] St. Luke apparently suggests as much when he mentions our Lady separately from the other holy women gathered in the Cenacle (Acts 1:14). But we cannot be sure of this because the very esteem accorded to Christ's relatives, which would soon be shown by the choice of "James, the brother of the Lord," as first Bishop of Jerusalem,[2] would have sufficed to give Mary a pre-eminent place in the primitive community.

Whatever Mary's precise role in the outpouring of the Holy Spirit on the infant Church may have been, we cannot doubt that her soul, always the object of God's favor and therefore in no need of a radical transformation, received a great increase in sanctity at Pentecost.

Mary, Fountain of Knowledge

Although our Lady never held a position of authority in the Church such as St. Peter and the other Apostles had received (Matt. 16:17 ff.; 18:18, etc.), she still exercised an unparalleled influence on it, even after the coming of the Holy Spirit and until the day of her death. She did so not only by her prayers and her qualities of mind and heart, but also by the information about her son that she alone was able to provide.

No doubt it was she who furnished most of the details from which the "infancy narratives" (Luke 1–2; Matt. 1–2) were composed, as St. Luke leads us to believe when he says that "Mary kept in mind all these words, pondering them in her heart" (Luke 2:19,51). And undoubtedly, after St. John had taken her into his care, it was she who communicated to him such a spirit of recollection that when he wrote his Gospel it was markedly "spiritual," as Clement of Alexandria observes.[3] In short, "when speaking of Jesus during her mortal life, Mary could say with greater authority and truth than the Apostles: 'We saw his glory—glory as of the only-begotten of the Father—full of grace and truth.'"[4]

Notes

1. Cf. *Maria, Etudes sur la Vierge*, vol. 6 (Paris, 1961), p. 48 f.
2. Cf. Eusebius, *Hist. Eccles.* III, 11.
3. Cf. Eusebius, *op. cit.*, VI, 14, 14.
4. J. J. Weber, *op. cit.*, p. 108; cf. John 1:14.

24

From Pentecost to Her Death

Mary's Last Years

THE SCRIPTURES are absolutely silent about Mary's life after Pentecost. But that is understandable because the sacred authors were then preoccupied with missionary expansion, as in the Acts of the Apostles, or with the education of newly established communities, as in the Apostles' letters and even the Apocalypse.

Marian piety began to be stressed with the rise of Christological thought. It arose about the end of the second century, when there appeared a number of apocryphal books whose authors hid their identity under the names of the Apostles or their disciples. These books claimed to be able to fill in the gaps in the Gospel narratives; where Mary was concerned, they were especially taken up with her background and early life, as in the *Protoevangelium of James,* or with the end of her life, as in the many versions of the *Transitus Mariae, The Falling Asleep of the Holy Mother of God.*[1] The various versions of the latter book, derived from a Greek original which dates back only as far as the fourth or fifth century, were still in vogue as late as the fourteenth century. It is not surprising that they differ considerably from each other. There was always a strong temptation for the editor or translator to add a few details of his own to feed the curiosity of the faithful. Consequently, if we were to believe them all, we should have to admit simultaneously that Mary lived for two, fifteen, twenty-two and twenty-four years after Pentecost. As a matter of fact, we find similar differences on this point even among the ancient ecclesiastical writers, who give figures ranging from two to thirty years; so that, in practice, we must admit that we simply don't know how long Mary lived.

However, we do not find it difficult to imagine the profound sentiments that animated our Lady during the period between Pentecost and her death. Obviously she must have suffered because she was no longer able to see her son close to her and because she knew that His mission was still not officially recognized by Israel, the Chosen People. But she also had many reasons to rejoice. She knew that she had no cause to fear for Him anymore. He had risen and was glorified forever. She could be united to Him in the Eucharist,[2] and she could follow happily the success of the infant Church. Like St. Paul, but to a greater degree, she no doubt lived more with the life of her son than with her own (cf. Gal. 2:20): she knew that she would rejoin Him some day and she longed with all her heart for that day to come (cf. Phil. 1:21 ff.; 2 Cor. 5:6 ff.). In a word, she possessed in a pre-eminent degree the inner dispositions of the perfect Christian.

Mary's Death

When defining the dogma of the Assumption on November 1, 1950, Pius XII did not settle the question of Mary's death. We all know that, by right, our Lady should not have been subject either to suffering or death, the consequences of sin, because she had been preserved from all sin, original and actual. But actually, as Simeon foretold (Luke 2:34), she did share her son's sufferings. Hence we can ask if, like her son, she too died. Few theologians maintain that she did not, and nearly all hold that she underwent the separation of soul and body to be fully associated in her son's redemption and to be brought even closer to us. However, they hasten to add that she did not die of illness or old age, but of love—and without pain. And they maintain that she did not undergo the corruption of the grave.

The apocryphal works mentioned above dwell at length on Mary's death and pretend to know the smallest details of it. According to them, our Lady breathed her last in her father's house in Jerusalem near the Mount of Olives, after many prayers, and in the presence of her Son, many angels, all but one of the Apostles, and numerous Christians. The Apostles had been miraculously brought together from their widespread mission fields (for example, St. John had been brought from Ephesus), and it was they who placed her holy remains in a new tomb in the valley of Cedron. Three days later, upon the arrival of Thomas, who had been providentially delayed this time, they found that her body had disappeared and were given a revelation of her triumphal ascent into heaven.[3] Artists have often derived inspiration from these descriptions.

Mary's Tomb

Both Jerusalem and Ephesus claim the honor of possessing our Lady's temporary resting place. Nowadays we know that it was only at the end of the sixth century that her "dormition" was first commemorated at Mount Sion in Jerusalem, and her burial at Gethsemane.[4] We also know the difficulties raised by the traditional texts that are advanced in favor of Ephesus: they are either not as clear as we should like or of rather late date. Both of these objections apply to the letter written by the Council of Ephesus to the clergy of Constantinople on June 23, 431, to notify them of the condemnation of Nestorius. Part of the letter is missing, so that it ends abruptly just at the point where it links the names of St. John and Mary with the city of Ephesus. The Council, it says, was held at Ephesus, "where John the Theologian and the Blessed Virgin Mary, Mother of God . . . "; then it breaks off short. We have to come down as far as the thirteenth century to find authors, either Syrian or Western, who suggest that the sentence should be completed as follows: "The Council was held at Ephesus where John the Theologian and the Blessed Virgin Mary, Mother of God, *came.*"[5] But we could also finish it like this: "The Council was held at Ephesus where John the Theologian and the Blessed Virgin Mary, Mother of God, *are honored.*" The latter suggestion has the advantage of fitting in very well with the recent discovery in Ephesus of the basilicas dating from the fourth century, one near the temple of Diana dedicated to St. John, and the second, near the ancient port, dedicated to Mary.[6]

While modern biblical scholars as a whole perfer to place our Lady's temporary tomb in Jerusalem, they do so not so much in the name of tradition as because of several texts from Scripture which, in their opinion, agree less easily with the Ephesian theory. They point out especially that St. John was in Jerusalem as late as the year 44 (Acts 12:1 ff.) and that he was there also about the year 50, at the Council of Jerusalem (Gal. 2:9). They think it equally unlikely that he went to Ephesus before 58, that is, until after St. Paul's declaration about confining his apostolate to those regions where the name of Christ had not yet been invoked (Rom. 15:20; cf. Acts 18:24 ff.; 19:1 ff.). They even think it probable that St. John's stay in Ephesus did not take place until after St. Paul's apostolate between 63 and 67, as described in the Pastoral Epistles. Finally, they believe that since our Lady had been born at least twenty years before the Christian era as usually reckoned, she would have been too old then to have ventured upon the journey to Ephesus.

Yet a learned Scripture commentator recently expressed a completely different opinion: "As mother of (Jesus) the condemned, Mary could not . . . very well have remained in Jerusalem when she was able to find suitable, safe refuge in an Essenian and Christian community at Ephesus. . . . This is more than possible; it is probable. . . . The silence of the texts on this subject would then be very satisfactorily explained, for it was fitting that the Christians should not talk too much about it in front of zealots and persecutors and in the midst of their own disagreements."[7]

Notes

1. Cf. *Maria, Etudes sur la Sainte Vierge*, vol. 6, p. 117 ff.
2. Cf. J. J. Weber, *Etudes Eucharistiques* (Paris, 1961), p. 43 ff.
3. Cf. *Transitus Mariae*, chaps. 3–18; see F. Amiot, *Evangiles Apocryphes* (Paris, 1952), p. 114 ff.; J. Hervieux, *Ce que l'Evangile ne dit pas* (Paris, 1958), p. 67 ff.

4. Cf. *Revue Biblique*, 1957, p. 146 f.

5. Cf. article by M. E. Delebecque in *Bulletin de l'Association Guillaume Budé*, 1956, p. 76–78; See C. Kopp, *Le tombeau de Marie, Jérusalem? Ephèse?* (Paderborn, 1955).

6. Cf. *Bible et Terre Sainte*, no. 13, 1958, p. 3 ff.; no. 51, 1962, p. 5 ff.; *Bible et Vie Chrétienne*, no. 38, 1961, p. 84 f.; Braun, *Jean le Théologien* (Paris, 1959), p. 365 ff.

7. H. Cazelles, in *Homme Nouveau*, Apr. 1, 1962, p. 10. The names and arguments of those who favor the tomb at Ephesus can be found in *Ecclesia, Lectures chrétiennes*, Aug., 1951, 1954, 1955. See also J. Euzet, *Historique de la Maison de la Sainte Vierge près d'Ephèse* (1891–1961): (Notre Dame d'Ephèse, Istanbul, 1961).

25

The Assumption

Definition of the Dogma

IN 1940 a study commission under the presidency of Msgr. Ottaviani began working to prepare for the dogmatic definition of the Assumption of our Lady. On May 1, 1946, Pius XII, in his encyclical *Deiparae Virginis,* asked all the bishops of the world about the belief of the faithful in Mary's Assumption. "We earnestly request you," he wrote, "to inform us of the devotion with which the clergy and people honor the Assumption of the Blessed Virgin Mary." On October 30, 1950, in his consistorial allocution *Nostis profecto,* preparatory to defining the dogma on the following day, he pointed out that the answers received had affirmed *the unanimous faith of pastors and faithful* in our Lady's Assumption and that, *consequently,* he had decided to proceed without further delay to the solemn definition of that dogma. "Since the Catholic Church as a whole," he added, "can neither deceive nor be deceived . . . , it follows that the truth of the Assumption, firmly believed by the Pastors and their people, is divinely revealed and can be defined by Our supreme authority."

On Wednesday November 1, 1950, at about 9:00 A.M., he proclaimed the dogma, which from then on became for us an object of faith. Standing in brilliant sunshine before a throng of nearly seven hundred prelates and 600,000 people gathered in St. Peter's Square, he read aloud the essential part of the Bull *Munificentissimus Deus:* "By the authority of our Lord Jesus Christ, of the Blessed Apostles Peter and Paul and by Our own authority, We proclaim, declare and define that it is a divinely revealed dogma that Mary, the Immaculate Mother of God, ever Virgin, when the course of her earthly life ended, was raised body and soul to the glory of heaven." The crowd, which had listened in deepest silence to these words, broke out into a storm of applause and cheering that culminated in a resounding *Te Deum.*

The Foundations of the Dogma

The new dogmatic definition was not an addition to the deposit of Revelation, which closed with the death of the last Apostle, but simply a clearer consciousness, on the Church's part, of another aspect of that Revelation which had been only implicit in the beginning. In fact, there is no precise statement of the Assumption in Scripture; it is found there only implicitly and virtually, and theological reasoning must be employed to deduce it from Holy Writ. But judging by the differences among the specialists before 1950 on the exact nature of this theological reasoning, we must admit that in last analysis the definition was based more on the enlightenment which the Holy Spirit always gives the Church in understanding revelation than on "the rather inflexible logic of theological deduction."[1]

From the fifth century on, the apocryphal writings described our Lady's death and glorification. They did not create belief in the Assumption but only supplied an imaginative expression "of the Christian people's unformulated conviction."[2] This conviction, first manifested externally in the early seventh century by the liturgical celebrations of August 15, was based upon the concept of Mary's divine maternity and the absolute holiness that such an incomparable dignity demands.[3]

That is how, before the definition of 1950, the unanimous faith of the pastors and faithful in the Assumption of the Blessed Virgin was formed, a faith that was profoundly accepted in the universal Church, as public devotion proved.[4] The faithful were convinced that, as it was with the son, so it must have been with the mother. They believed that since Mary had been preserved from Original Sin through the foreseen merits of her son, so she must have escaped the consequences of that sin, such as the body's being turned to dust and remaining in the state of death until the end of time. Our Lord had not willed this to happen to His own body; so the faithful believed that His filial love would not have allowed Him to refuse His mother the privilege of the Assumption, the logical culmination of all the other privileges with which He had already honored her.

Consequences of the Dogma

The definition came at the right moment. At a time when men had decided that their destiny was confined to this earth, it was fitting that a perspective should be opened on heaven. At an hour when men had begun to doubt and even to despair of themselves, it was fitting to affirm the perfect success of grace in Mary, who had been glorified in soul and body. In an age when false mysticism was trying to raise the veil on life beyond the tomb, it was necessary to stress our last end. In a world where worship of the body had only resulted in profanation of it, men had to be reminded that the body is the temple of the Holy Ghost and that God wishes to glorify it. By throwing light upon the meaning of man, the world, and history, and by anticipating the end of all three, the Assumption foreshadowed the state of humanity in a renewed world. Since man was promised such a destiny, the Assumption gave him a better grasp of the fact that he is not a mere creature of pointless passion or the end-product of material conditions. When we think of Mary's triumph, we think also of our own, which is attained in two steps: first, death loses some of its terror for us, and then, illuminated by the rays of eternal life, it becomes in a way even desirable.

Finally, through this dogma we learn that Mary belongs to the present as well as the past, that in a sense she is our contemporary, and that there exists between her, our mother, and us, her children, a real, living, supernatural relationship from which we can derive courage and confidence.

Notes

1. H. Holstein in *Maria, Etudes sur la Vierge,* vol. 6 (1961), p. 241 ff.
2. *Ibid.,* p. 279.
3. Cf. *ibid.,* p. 277.
4. Cf. *ibid.,* p. 286 f.

26

Mary in the Apocalypse

The Apocalypse

IN THE YEAR 95, while exiled on the island of Patmos some sixty miles out from Ephesus, St. John wrote the Apocalypse or "Revelation," one of the most mysterious books in the Bible. His purpose was to reveal things that hitherto had been known only to God, especially in regard to what lay in store for the Church and its members until the end of the world. In doing so he used a specialized language that gave to details and even to whole descriptive passages a *symbolic* value different from their ordinary meaning. As a result of careful study of the Bible and the contemporary Jewish literature, from which an appreciable part of this specialized language was derived, at least the general meaning of the book is clear.

The Apostle wrote with the object of strengthening the Christians' faith and reviving their hope. He knew the dangers of all kinds that threatened them—persecution by the officials of the Roman Empire, betrayal by informers, the teaching of false apostles, absorption into pagan cults, the tyrannical demands of the state religion. In a succession of more or less parallel visions and with a vivid form of imagery that was very much in vogue at the time, he showed them that even these multiple dangers could not injure the true welfare of the Christian or impede the Church's progress toward its final triumph. He taught them that God and the glorified Christ reign from heaven on high and personally direct the events of history—past, present and future (chaps. 1–5). They know all things, especially the vain attacks on the Church by the politico-religious forces which have put themselves at the service of Satan (chaps. 6–16); although They are firmly determined to crush these forces, They would tolerate them while waiting for the number of the elect to be completed (*ibid.*); nevertheless, They would soon annihilate the power of Rome the persecutor (chaps. 17–18); after a long period of peace granted to the Church and a brief renewal of attacks by the devil, They would destroy forever the forces of evil by the final battle, the last judgment, (chaps. 20–21) and the foundation of the city of the elect (chaps. 21–22).

The Vision of the Woman and the Dragon

Among the descriptions which the Apocalypse gives of the attacks directed against the Church, there is one which, according to quite a large number of authors, is concerned with the Blessed Virgin. However, before we discuss it, let us review the main part of the description:

"And a great sign appeared in heaven: a woman clothed

with the sun, and the moon was under her feet, and upon her head a crown of twelve stars. And being with child, she cried out in her travail and was in the anguish of delivery. And another sign was seen in heaven, and behold a great red dragon having seven heads and ten horns, and upon his heads seven diadems. . . . The ancient serpent, he who is called the devil and Satan . . . , stood before the woman who was about to bring forth, that when she had brought forth he might devour her son. And she brought forth a male child, who is to rule all nations with a rod of iron; and her child was caught up to God and his throne. And the woman fled into the wilderness, where she has a place prepared by God, that there they may nourish her a thousand, two hundred and sixty days. . . . And the serpent cast out of his mouth after the woman water like a river, that he might cause her to be carried away by the river. And the earth helped the woman, and the earth opened her mouth and swallowed up the river that the dragon had cast out of his mouth. And the dragon was angered at the woman, and went away to wage war with the rest of her offspring, who keep the commandments of God, and hold fast the testimony of Jesus" (chap. 12:1–6, 9, 15–17).

The Woman, a Symbol of God's People

We have not far to search in order to find what the dragon represents in this description, for St. John himself tells us that it is "the ancient serpent . . . , the devil . . . Satan." We also learn eventually (Apoc. 17:9 ff.) that the dragon's heads and diadems simply mean the various worldly powers that put themselves at his service (Apoc. 13:1 ff.). On the other hand, however, we are not directly told the symbolism of the woman surrounded by the heavenly bodies and persecuted by Satan; we perceive it only after a rather lengthy examination of the sacred texts, an examination which we must abbreviate here.

In other passages in the Apocalypse, "the woman" is indubitably the symbol of a group; for example, the tyrannical Roman Empire (chaps. 17–18), or the Church triumphant, the Spouse of Christ (19:7; 21:2). This is also true in the Old Testament and in Judaism in general: "There the woman primarily symbolizes God's people, who begot the Messias and the messianic race" (M. E. Boismard).[1] Consequently, we are inclined to believe that it is the same in the Apocalypse.

But what group does the Apocalypse refer to in the passage we have just quoted? Primarily the group that is preparing to give birth to the Messias (12:2, 4 f.), that is, ancient Israel, the Chosen People before the coming of Christ. There can be no doubt as to the identity of the male child whose birth the woman is expecting at any moment, for he is described in the very terms that the psalmist used to point out the leader of a renewed Israel, the one who "shall rule them with an iron rod" (Ps. 2:9). Furthermore, the Apocalypse later applies this description to the glorified Christ, the conqueror of the forces of evil (19:15; cf. 2:27). Long before the coming of her child the Messias, the woman (the group, the Chosen People) was acquainted with suffering and the devil's attacks in the form of war, exile, and persecutions.

The group envisaged here also includes the Church of Christ, the new Israel, which is an extension of the old. For the woman survives until the coming and even the glorious ascension of her male child, the Messias (12:5 f.), and she has other children "who keep the commandments of God, and hold fast the testimony of Jesus" (12:17). The Church-community and its descendants also suffer the attacks of

Satan (12:6, 13 ff.), but only for a time, the symbolical period mentioned by Daniel (7:25; 12:7) . . . "a thousand two hundred and sixty days" (Apoc. 12:6; cf. 11:3), or "a time and times and a half time" (Apoc. 12:14). During the whole course of these attacks, God gives the group (the Church) the means of survival, arranging a refuge for it and feeding it (12:6, 14). He even gives the children of the woman (the Church) the power to triumph spiritually over the persecutor "through the blood of the Lamb and through the word of their (own) witness" (12:11). In the chapters that follow (chaps. 13 ff.), the Apostle describes at length these attacks of the devil, or rather the attacks of his earthly agents.

We should note in passing that the woman (the People of God), surrounded by heavenly bodies (12:1), is a reminder of the splendors of the heavenly Spouse (Jerusalem; 21:1 ff.), and symbolizes very accurately the incomparable grandeur which she possesses in God's eyes and which surpasses that of all creation (cf. Ps. 104: 2; Cant. 6:10; Gen. 37:9).

The Woman, a Symbol of Mary

For some Catholic authors, both ancient and modern,[2] the symbolism of the woman in our text can be none other than that which we have just described. According to them, it is unthinkable that St. John would have wished to extend the symbolism to Mary because several parts of the description cannot be made to fit her, such as the pains of childbirth, the flight into the wilderness, and the woman's numerous descendants. Hence the text can be applied to the Blessed Virgin only in an accommodated sense, that is, to the extent that some elements can be lifted out of their context and adapted to her.

Other Catholic authors do not accept this point of view[3]

and hold that the symbolism of the woman applies, in the literal sense, both to the People of God and to the Blessed Virgin. According to them

John saw fit to describe the one by using characteristics proper to the other. The procedure was a usual one, and it brings out the fact that there is a relationship of type between two subjects. For example, in chapter six of St. John's Gospel, "the bread of life" is at once the manna, faith, and the sacrament of the Eucharist. Here (in the Apocalypse) John again parallels Luke: he shows the Blessed Virgin as the eschatological completion of Israel, the daughter of Sion giving birth to the Savior. (R. Laurentin)

These authors point out that in the text in question the pains of childbirth are metaphorical, as is the flight into the wilderness, so that there is no reason why they should not be applied to Mary, the Mother of Sorrows—especially on Calvary, and the Mother most pure, preserved from the attacks of the devil.

They also make much of the fact that Mary gave birth to the Messias more directly and concretely than did ancient Israel; that, like the new Israel, the Church, she is the spiritual mother of every disciple of Jesus (cf. John 19:25 ff.), so that it is not out of place to speak of her other offspring; that her greatness, now emphasized by the dogma of the Assumption, is in harmony with the appearance of the woman of the Apocalypse, surrounded by stars and raised aloft on the wings of a great eagle (Apoc. 12:14).

Finally, these authors hold that the woman of the Apocalypse is described in relation to Eve, the first woman, tempted by the ancient serpent, condemned to give birth in pain and, with her children, to be the target of Satan's hatred (Gen. 3:1 ff.). And since, according to them, Eve certainly prefigured Mary—a conclusion which others dispute—they deduce that the woman of the Apocalypse truly symbolizes Mary in the literal sense.

At all events, it is certain that the liturgy and religious art are perfectly correct in applying to our Lady several of the elements in the description which we quoted at the beginning of this chapter, "because between Mary and the body of the faithful there exists not only a bond or origin, but a profound analogy. Like ancient Israel . . . , Mary has given birth to the Messias, and, like the Church, she is the Mother of every disciple of Jesus. Her personal destiny is identified with that of Israel, ancient and new, as a whole."[4]

Notes

1. Cf. 4 Esdras 9:38; 10:59. See *Introduction à la Bible* (Paris, 1959), vol. 2, p. 738; *Cahiers Evangile*, no. 13, pp. 16–23; J. J. Weber, *op. cit.*, p. 118.

2. Cf. *Mélanges A. Robert*, p. 512, note 1; *Introduction à la Bible*, vol. 2, p. 737 f.; *Maria*, vol. 6, p. 62, note 1.

3. Cf. R. Laurentin, *Court Traité de Théologie Mariale* (1959), p. 33 ff.; *Luc I–II*, p. 83 ff.; J. J. Weber, *La Vierge Marie dans le Nouveau Testament*, p. 118 ff. See A. Feuillet, *Etudes Johanniques* (Paris, 1962), p. 287 ff.

4. H. Troadec, *Le Message de Saint Jean* (Mame, 1962), p. 182.

27

Woman: Our Lord's Teaching

Preliminary Remarks

IN THE JEWISH WORLD reflected in the New Testament, a woman lived under substantially the same conditions as in Old Testament times.

As a child, she was the center of loving care (Mark 5:23; 35 ff.; cf. 7:25 ff.; Luke 18:15); and as a marriageable girl she was subject to her father's authority (1 Cor. 7:3 ff.). But as a wife, her life was one of unending toil (Matt. 24:41; 13:33; Luke 10:40; 15:8 ff.); she lived in fear of being barren and hence despised (Luke 1:25), of being accused of adultery and put to death (John 8:3 ff.; cf. Matt. 1:19), or of being repudiated by her husband and, at the very least, losing her home (Matt. 19:1 ff.; 5:32). As a widow, she was a prey to poverty (Luke 21:1 ff.; Acts 6:1; 11:39 ff.; 1 Tim.

5:5 ff.), to exploitation by swindlers (Mark 12:40), to the loss of her children (Luke 7:12f.), to forgetfulness on the part of her family (Mark 7:9ff.; 1 Tim. 5:4, 8, 26), to prostitution (Luke 7:37; Matt. 21:31f.; John 4:17f.; 1 Tim. 5:5, 6, 15), and perhaps even to slavery (Acts 16:16; 1 Cor. 7:17ff.). Often her only hope was to remarry (John 4:17; 1 Tim. 5:11 ff.) or to benefit by the provisions of the levirate law (Matt. 22:2, 23).

But there is no need to go on since we have already discussed this matter. Rather, in the short space available, we shall try to discover from the New Testament the improvements which the last part of Revelation brought about in women's life (cf. Matt. 5:17; Hebr. 1:1f.). To do so, we shall examine our Lord's teaching on the role of women, and then the teaching of the Apostles on the same subject.

Our Lord's Teaching

An attentive reading of the Gospels reveals that Christ left us no explicit or direct teaching on the nature and role of women. Here, as in many other cases, He taught us only by means of the attitudes He adopted and the reflections which circumstances suggested to Him. This is primarily due to the fact that, as the Word Incarnate, He Himself is the Way, the Truth and the Life (John 1:4ff.; 14:6), the Light that enlightens all men (John 1:9; 8:12). But undoubtedly there were also more immediate reasons for His method, such as the inadvisability of suddenly disrupting the prevailing customs and the need to adapt His teaching to the mentality of His audience.

We shall, then, seek to determine His thoughts on the nature and role of women by examining His attitudes and His occasional declarations on the matter.

It quickly becomes evident that in our Lord's eyes

women are equal to men both from the natural and the supernatural point of view.[1] While taking fully into account the profound differences between the sexes (cf. Matt. 22:30; 5:28; John 4:27 . . .), He acknowledged in effect that women, just as men, possess a rational soul and that they are destined for the same life of grace and glory.

Fundamentally Equal by Nature

In replying to a question about divorce, Christ referred to Genesis (1:27) to remind His listeners that God created the same human nature, "male and female" (Matt. 19:4).

The Incarnation itself gives exalted testimony that this is so, for it was from the female sex alone that Christ received His body as a man. Here is what St. Augustine said about the matter:

Christ willed to receive in Himself the masculine sex and deigned to honor in His Mother the feminine sex. . . . If He had become man without the help of the female sex, woman would have despaired of herself, the more so since it was she who had brought about the man's fall. But (Christ) has honored both sexes, He has been attentive to both and has taken care of both. He was born of woman. . . . May the two sexes hasten together toward salvation! Both men and women must come, for in the faith there is neither man nor woman.[2]

At the finding in the Temple Jesus addressed Mary *and* Joseph, and afterwards He was subject to both of them (Luke 2:49, 51). The use of the plural of the verbs and pronouns indicates that He regarded both Mary's and Joseph's higher faculties, their intellects and wills, as being on the same plane. And we should not forget that in Nazareth the angel Gabriel took account of Mary's objection and did not leave until he had received her consent (Luke 1:34 f., 38).

During His public life our Lord did not hesitate to spend some of His short, precious time speaking to and conversing with women . . . with His mother, of course (John 2:4), but also with Lazarus's two sisters (Luke 10:38 ff.), with sinful women (John 8:10 ff.; Luke 7:49), heretics (John 4:7 ff.), and pagans (Mark 7:25 ff.). He made no distinction between these women and men like Nathanael (John 1: 47 ff.) or Nicodemus (John 3:1 ff.) as regards their mental faculties.

He took account of women's requests and needs in the same way as He did those of men, even when He had to work the greatest miracles to do so. In Cana He did what His mother suggested (John 2:4 ff.). In Phoenicia He acceded to the prayer of the woman whom His disciples wanted to send away (Matt. 15:22 ff.). At Bethany He raised His friend Lazarus in answer to appeals of Martha and Mary (John 11; 3, 20 ff.). In Galilee He healed the poor woman who was so shy about asking to be cured of a hemorrhage (Mark 5:25). He took pity on the widow at Naim who had not even asked Him for help (Luke 7:11 ff.). He who had proclaimed that the Sabbath was made for men (Mark 2:27) did not hesitate to cure on that day a woman who had been bent over for eighteen years (Luke 13:10 ff.). Even when He was at the point of death on the cross, He saw to His mother's future by confiding her to His beloved disciple (John 19:26 ff.). He was never indifferent to any woman's distress, as we can see from His stern words to the Pharisees, who exploited widows (Mark 12:40), and from His parable of the widow and the unjust judge (Luke 18:2 ff.). In short, there is nothing in our Lord's conduct to indicate that He admitted the least essential difference between men and women.

As a matter of fact, far from admitting that such a

difference existed, He held that women were capable of the same moral dispositions as men, and He made the same demands of them. He told the woman caught in adultery to sin no more (John 8:11), just as He had done with the paralytic at the pool of Bethsaida (John 5:14). He wished that He could find in the Pharisees as much faith and charity as He had in the notoriously sinful woman who came to ask his forgiveness (Luke 7:36 ff.), or in the poor widow donating to the Temple the little she had to live on (Luke 21:1 ff.; cf. 11:31 f.). He was indignant with the disciples for not appreciating the gesture made by those mothers who brought their children to be blessed (Mark 10:13 ff.). He placed Mary of Bethany's loving prodigality far above Judas's avarice (John 12:3 ff.). On the road to Calvary, despite the insults of the men and the weight of the cross, He showed that He appreciated the compassion which the pious women had for Him and He paused to console them (Luke 23:37 ff.). On the second day after His death, while the Apostles were still in hiding, He made known His Resurrection to the women who had not been afraid to come and pay their last respects to Him (Mark 16:1 ff.; John 20:11 ff.).

He valued woman's moral dispositions more highly than any honor that was proper to her sex, even motherhood. Thus He proclaimed that His own mother was more blessed for having believed and lived a holy life than for having given birth to Him and nursed Him (Luke 11:27 f.). He did not accede to Martha's request, when she was so over-solicitous in preparing a meal that she wanted to take her sister away from listening to the Word (Luke 10:38 ff.). And He so inspired the Samaritan woman that she left her pitcher at the well and forgot the fatigue of drawing the water (John 4:28, 15).

Equality in Supernatural Destiny

Our Lord's attitude toward women reflected His views on their supernatural destiny: they were made for the life of grace and eternal glory, just as men were. When He preached, His announcement of salvation and His calls to conversion were addressed to all men and to all women.

Even more, so that His women listeners would grasp His meaning more easily, He went to great pains to use examples taken from their daily life (Mark 2:21; 13:17; Luke 15:8 f.; 17:35; Matt. 13:33). By so doing He caught and held their attention, stirring them to enthusiasm if not always to conversion (Luke 10:39; 11:27).[3] In the parable of the ten virgins, He specified that if they were to gain entry to the eternal wedding feast, they would have to display the required dispositions on earth (Matt. 25:1 ff.).

He let it be clearly understood that being male or female was quite secondary as regards eternity and the life of grace, and that sex was not a factor in determining who were His true disciples: "Who are my mother and my brethren. . . ? Whoever does the will of God, he is my brother and sister and mother" (Mark 3:33; Luke 11:27 f.; Matt. 7:21 ff.). Nor would it enter into account at the Last Judgment: "Come, blessed of my Father, take possession of the kingdom prepared for you . . . ; for I was hungry and you gave me to eat; I was thirsty and you gave me to drink . . ." (Matt. 25:34 f.). Difference of sex loses all importance in the next life where "they will neither marry nor be given in marriage but are as the angels of God in heaven" (Matt. 22:30). That is why our Lord told the obstinately self-righteous Pharisees that even harlots who repented would enter the kingdom of God before them (Matt. 21:31 f.). In saying so, He was probably thinking of the Samaritan woman who believed so quickly in

Him; of the sinful woman and her gesture of repentance in the house of Simon the leper; of the possessed women whom He had freed from evil spirits and who then put themselves at His service (Luke 8:2f.; Mark 16:9).

Christ's Teaching on Women's Role

We shall now try to determine what our Lord's thought was on the role that women must play in life. Here again we find that He left us no explicit teaching and that we must discover His doctrine from the facts provided by the Gospel. It matters little whether these facts are entirely new or whether we may have already examined them from another angle. The main thing is to ascertain Christ's teaching.

First, our Lord wanted women to be motherly, as is clear from the number of times His actions showed His respect for and encouragement of their maternal feelings. He was kind and considerate to His own mother (John 2:1 ff.; 19:26 f.); He took pity on the Canaanite woman who begged Him to cure her daughter (Matt. 15:22 ff.) and on the widow at Naim who was on the way to bury her only son. He was especially kind to those women who asked Him to bless their children, and He allowed the mothers of several of the disciples to join His small band of companions (Matt. 27:56). He replied courteously to the pretentious request made by the mother of James and John, the sons of Zebedee (Matt. 20:30 ff.); and He was solicitous in expressing His pity for the children of the pious women of Jerusalem (Luke 23:28).

Christ also wanted women to be good housekeepers, as is proved to a certain extent by all the similes and metaphors that He took from the housewife's daily routine, which we have already mentioned. Then, too, there is the miracle that He worked at Cana in answer to His mother's request, when she wished to ensure that nothing would be lacking; the cure of St. Peter's mother-in-law, so that she was able to get up and wait on Him (Mark 1:31); the help He accepted from the holy women among His followers (Luke 8:3); the hospitality He gladly received at the house of Martha and Mary. However, He did not wish the management of a household to become mere showing-off and to be so obsessive that it worked against the good of the soul; that is clear from the answer He gave Martha (Luke 10:41).

Our Lord wanted women to have a chance to learn, at least in religious matters; otherwise how explain the care He took to preach to them, His solicitude in adapting His doctrine to their understanding, the moral character that He demanded of them and that was the condition for attaining their real destiny? The completely biblical nature of the language which the angel Gabriel used at the Annunciation, and our Lady's own Magnificat, so full of echoes from the inspired books, reveal a little of Mary's religious culture. In fact, at that period and in the Jewish atmosphere then prevailing in Palestine, there could scarcely have been question of any other kind of culture. Hellenism was still foreign even to the educated rabbis.[4] The parable of the talents (Matt. 25:14; cf. Luke 19:11 ff.), no doubt addressed to men and to women, is confirmation that our Lord wished women to possess religious perfection. The parable even leads us to believe that when circumstances were suitable, He favored the development of supplementary talents.

There is one domain, however, into which He did not permit women to intrude, and that is the *administration of His Church*. There were no women among His disciples and there were none especially among His Apostles, who were destined to be the leaders in the Church (Mark 3:13 ff.; John 1:35 ff., etc.). Only men took part in the temporary

mission in Galilee (Matt. 10:1 ff.; Luke 10:1 ff.); received
special instruction (Mark 4:11, 34; 9:30 ff.); were given
the mission of preaching the Gospel to every nation (Matt.
28:16 ff.; Acts 1:8); and were entrusted with the perpetua-
tion of the Eucharist (Luke 22:19; 1 Cor. 11:24 f.). Moreover, it is hard to see any basis for the opinion, which some
express, that perhaps one day women will attain the priestly
office.[5]

But we must recognize the fact that, apart from the case
of the priesthood, our Lord did not by any means intend to
deprive His Church of women's powerful assistance. Quite
the opposite is true. For did not He, the founder of the
Church, come into the world through Mary? Was it not also
through Mary that He exercised the first visible apostolate
of His life at the Visitation when, at the sound of our Lady's
voice, John the Baptist leaped for joy and Elizabeth was
enlightened by the Holy Spirit (Luke 1:41, 44)? At the
wedding in Cana He waited for Mary to intervene before He
worked the miracle that would strengthen His first disciples'
faith in Him as the Messias (John 2:11). During His public
life He accepted and even sought material assistance from
His first women converts, assistance which allowed Him to
extend His missionary activity. On the cross He gave Mary
as a mother to St. John, who was to become the most sublime
of the Evangelists. Two days later He chose some of the
holy women to be the first ones to bring the news of His
Resurrection to the very Apostles themselves (Mark 16:7;
Luke 24:9; John 20:17 f.). And finally, on Pentecost He
sent the Holy Spirit, the Soul of His Church, to the Twelve,
who were gathered around Mary in the Cenacle (Acts 1:14).[6]

Besides improving woman's role in family life, our Lord
encouraged her to undertake the apostolic activity that He
expected of her. He desired that she should no longer be

man's victim or plaything; but since every society must have a head if it is to survive, He still upheld the authority of the husband and father. This is clear from His numerous parables concerning the head of a household (Matt. 21:28 ff.; Luke 11:11; 15:12 ff., etc.), and the texts in which we find that, according to God's own will, all decisions regarding the Holy Family devolved upon St. Joseph (Matt. 1:20 f., 25; 2:13, 19, 22; Luke 2:4 f., 48).

But Christ placed the authority of God, the Heavenly Father of all, beside and *above* this earthly authority (Matt. 23:9). In any case of conflict, the Father's will must come first: His will must be done on earth as it is in heaven (Matt. 6:10); we must always be obedient to it if we are to be worthy of Christ and deserve the name of disciple (Matt. 10:35 ff.; Mark 10:29 ff.; Luke 9:59; 14:26). These liberating principles were to be frequently applied in cases of conversion (Matt. 10:35 ff.) or vocation to virginity (Matt. 19:10 ff.). The *husband's authority* ceased to be absolute. Our Lord abolished divorce and re-established the original indissolubility of the marriage bond: "Whoever puts away his wife . . . , and marries another, commits adultery" (Matt. 19:5 ff.; Gen. 2:24).[7] That was the end of the masculine privilege conceded by the Law of Moses (Deut. 24:1 ff.): the husband could now become guilty of adultery against his wife, who henceforth possessed an inalienable right, equal to that of her husband. As a result, her security and her sphere of action increased tenfold.

Let us end our enquiry here, for brief though it has been, it has sufficed to provide us with the essential elements in our Lord's teaching on woman's nature and role; and it has allowed us to admire the beauty of God's Providence as it works in the world of creation.

Notes

1. Cf. *Nouvelle Revue Théologique*, 1957, p. 923 ff., art. by H. Rondet: "Eléments pour une théologie de la femme."
2. Migne, P.L., vol. 6, p. 935, quoted by Van der Meer, *Saint Augustin, pasteur d'âmes* (Alsatia, 1955), vol. 2, p. 311.
3. Cf. *Les Cahiers du Clergé Rural*, no. 197, Apr., 1958, p. 200; *La Pédagogie du Christ* (Paris, 1961), p. 43 f.
4. Cf. S. Ricciotti, *Saint Paul the Apostle* (Milwaukee, Bruce, 1953), p. 35 ff.
5. Cf. E. Stein, *La destinée de la femme; Lumière et Vie*, no. 43, July–Aug., 1959, p. 65 ff., art. by F. R. Refoulé: "Les femmes-prêtres en Suède."
6. Cf. H. Rondet, *loc. cit.*, p. 924.
7. Cf. DBS, art. on "Mariage," pp. 921–935.

28

Woman: the Apostles' Teaching

Preliminary Remarks

THE APOSTLES, instructed in all things by the Holy Spirit (John 14:26; 16:12 f.; 20:22), necessarily repeated their Master's teaching, and perhaps even enriched it here and there because He had not been able to communicate all His doctrine to them before Pentecost (John 16:12). We shall see that this is so when we examine the writings of the Apostles, among which we must include the four Gospels since all four reproduce the Apostles' preaching. Here again we shall find what we seek in the Apostles' attitudes and in the implications of what they say, rather than in outright statements, although we shall discover explicit instructions, too, particularly in St. Paul's epistles.

Fundamentally Equal by Nature

As in the previous chapter, we shall begin by enquiring into the Apostles' teaching about woman's nature and destiny. In his First Epistle to the Corinthians, St. Paul at first glance seems to teach that women are by nature inferior to men (1 Cor. 11:3 ff.). However, he is thinking only of woman's *hierarchical* inferiority, of her subordination to authority, and is concerned merely with the role she must play and not with her very nature. While he teaches that she should show her subordination by covering her head at liturgical functions, he goes on to state clearly the natural equality of the sexes: "Yet neither is man independent of woman, nor woman independent of man in the Lord. For as the woman is from the man, so also is the man through the woman, but all things are from God" (1 Cor. 11:11 f.).

Elsewhere, the Apostle tells us that "when the fullness of time came, God sent his Son, born of a woman" (Gal. 4:4). Many authors believe that we must see in this text an indication of Mary's virginal conception of Christ and not merely the bald statement that the Son of God became man. If these authors are right, then the text is simply an indirect repetition of St. Paul's words quoted above.

As well as relying on positive declarations, we must have recourse especially to the attitude of the Apostles toward women. In doing so, we shall see that they followed in their Master's footsteps, being concerned about women as much as about men and showing by their actions that the members of both sexes possess essentially the same intellects and wills. Here are some examples: St. Peter allowed women to be present in the Cenacle (Acts 1:14); he mentioned daughters and maidservants in his sermons (Acts 2:17 f.); he took care to see that the widows of the Hellenists were well treated

(Acts 6:1 ff.); he raised Tabitha from the dead to restore her to her good works among the poor Christians of Joppa (Acts 9:36 ff.); he demanded exemplary conduct from wives (1 Pet. 3:1 ff.); and he punished Sapphira with death because she lied (Acts 5:7 ff.).

When the opportunity arose, St. Paul spoke to audiences of women (Acts 16:13 f.; 17:4, 12; 18:3, 18; 24:24; 26: 23 ff.); treated women with deference, and greeted them by name in his epistles (1 Cor. 16:19; Rom. 16:1 ff.; 2 Tim. 1:5; 4:19, 21); asked his disciples to do the same (Philipp. 4:3; 1 Tim. 5:2); commended Christian women travelers (Rom. 16:1 f.), and especially helpless widows (1 Tim. 5:3 ff.), to the care of the communities; demanded that all, both men and women, flee vice and practise virtue (Philipp. 4:2; 1 Tim. 5:6, 12 f.; 2 Tim. 3:6 ff.; 1 Thess. 4:1 ff.); and placed a greater value upon virtue than upon motherhood itself (1 Tim. 2:15).

The other Apostles or their disciples, who left writings behind them, testify to the same effect, thus proving that they did not believe that woman was by nature inferior to man. The author of the Epistle to the Hebrews praises simultaneously the heroes and heroines of the Old Testament (Hebr. 11:11 ff.). The first three Evangelists, St. Luke even more than the others, record a teaching tradition in which women had a large part. From these sources we learn that in the first Christian gatherings in Palestine (Matthew), Rome (Mark) and Greece (Luke) frequent mention was made of the Blessed Virgin, Elizabeth, Anna the prophetess, the sisters of Lazarus, Mary Magdalene, and many other women (Luke 7:11 ff., 36 ff.; 8:2 f.; 9:31; 23:55 ff., etc.); and we find that their virtues were pointed out so as to inspire others to imitate them or, more rarely, that the malice of evil women was cited in order to turn others away from sin

(Mark 6:22 ff.; Acts 13:50). Moreover, great emphasis was placed on the favors which Christ or His Father had bestowed on these holy women. In short, women were not regarded as a negligible part of the Church; rather, efforts were made to reinstate them in the eyes of a world that underrated them.

St. John acted in the same way in the churches of Asia Minor. His teaching, which we find in the fourth Gospel, also speaks about the Blessed Virgin, the sisters of Lazarus, Mary Magdalene, the Samaritan woman, and the woman caught in adultery: each reference is a reminder of womanly virtue or of our Lord's consideration for the weaker sex.

While it is not certain that St. John was alluding to our Lady in his description of the woman adorned with the sun, moon, and stars (Apoc. 12:1 ff.), we do know that he spoke of the Church as a woman, a fact eloquent enough in itself. He repeated this figure of speech later when he wrote about the Church as the ideal spouse of Christ, the Lamb of God (Apoc. 19:7 f.; 21:2 f., 9 ff.; 2 John 1:13).

Equality in Supernatural Destiny

The Apostles' thought on woman's supernatural destiny did not differ from our Lord's, anymore than did their views on her nature and role. There is no room for doubt on this point because, judging by the Gospels, which contain their basic teaching, the Apostles faithfully repeated here, as elsewhere, the doctrine they had received from Christ. However, although we are far from having made sufficient use here of the Gospels as the depositories of the Apostles' teaching, we shall not go back to examine them. We shall content ourselves with having directed attention to this aspect of them, and shall turn instead to the other apostolic texts.

St. Peter held that the life of grace or, as he called it, partaking of the divine nature (2 Pet. 1:4), was the prerogative of Christian women as well as of Christian men. He proclaimed this teaching on Pentecost day, quoting the prophet Joel on the coming of the Holy Spirit into the hearts of God's servants and handmaids, His sons and daughters (Acts 2:17 f.). He preached it to those husbands who were little inclined to respect their wives: "The woman . . . (is) co-heir of the grace of life" (1 Pet. 3:7). He loved to recall how the men and the women who had listened to him in the house of Cornelius the centurion had received an outpouring of God's gifts, even before he had decided whether or not to baptize them (Acts 10:44 ff.; 11:15 ff.; 15:8 ff.). And he judged that Sapphira, like her husband Ananias before her, had lied to the Holy Spirit Himself, allowing Satan to enter her heart (Acts 5:3, 9).

St. Paul, who before his conversion had persecuted Christians of both sexes (Acts 9:2; 22:4), was given a sudden revelation in his vision on the road to Damascus. He discovered that there was a very close, mysterious bond between the risen Christ and these Christian men and women (Acts 9:4; 22:7; 26:14). When he learned shortly afterward about the Savior's redemption of men and experienced it in a very personal way (Acts 9:17 f.; Gal. 2:20; Philipp. 1:21), he saw the source of that bond. It is the very life of Christ— a life communicated by His Spirit (Rom. 8:9 f.) to every Christian at the moment of baptism (Rom. 6:3 ff.; Tit. 3:5 f.) and continually increased by the exercise of charity (1 Cor. 13:1 ff.; Ephes. 4:16; 2:9), a life that remains after death because the soul is then face to face with the Lord (1 Cor. 13:12; Philipp. 1:23). From then on, in St. Paul's eyes, Christ and Christians became one and the same "body" through which the same life flowed (1 Cor. 12:12 f., 27).

When he contemplated this union, of which Christ is the

principle (Ephes. 1:22 f.; Col. 1:18), he saw that distinctions of race, sex, and social status are wiped out: "There is neither Jew nor Greek; there is neither slave nor freeman; there is neither male nor female. For you are all one in Christ Jesus" (Gal. 3:28; Col. 3:11; 1 Cor. 12:13).

By virtue of this unity, to which all must contribute (Ephes. 4:1 ff.), he gave the name of brothers and sisters to Christian men and women, and he called Christ Himself "the firstborn among many brethren" (1 Thess. 4:10; Rom. 16:13; 8:29). Knowing that God wishes all men to be saved, he longed for the time when this multitude would grow as large as the universe (1 Tim. 2:4; Rom. 11:11 ff.). While he waited for that day to come, he preached to women, had them baptized, exhorted them to become holy and not to commit sin for fear that they might die to the life of grace (Acts 16:15; 1 Cor. 7:5, 25 ff.; 1 Tim. 3:11; 5:5 ff.).

The author of the Epistle to the Hebrews places in heaven the men and women of the Old Testament who had lived a life of faith (Hebr. 11:40). They are there on high, he says, as "a cloud of witnesses" to our journey towards Christ (Hebr. 12: ff.). St. John, too, speaks about the saints of heaven, both men and women, as an immense crowd gathered from every part of the world and impossible to count (Apoc. 7:9; 14:1 ff.).

Woman's Role

One question yet remains: what was the Apostles' idea of woman's role? St. Peter and particularly St. Paul supply us with the elements of the answer.

On two occasions St. Peter acted in such a way as to show that he did not even consider that women should have a place in the Catholic hierarchy. Once, when it was a question of filling Judas's place among the Twelve Apostles, and again at the election of deacons to help the Apostles, he required the choice to be made from among the men (Acts 1:21; 6:3). However, he well understood that women did have a part to play in the apostolate. He counted greatly on the edifying conduct of wives to bring about the conversion of their husbands (1 Pet. 3:1 ff.); he asked all the faithful to join together in their "spiritual sacrifices" for the building up of the people of God (1 Pet. 2:5). He relied upon the material assistance of the Christian women who made their houses available for the liturgical gatherings (Acts 12:1 ff.), or who accompanied him on his missions (1 Cor. 9:5). And no doubt he remembered gratefully his mother-in-law's hospitality (Mark 1:31). As regards married life, he, too, maintained the principle that the wife is subject to her husband (1 Pet. 3:1).

St. Paul formally excluded women from the ecclesiastical hierarchy. Relying on the common practice in the communities in Palestine and elsewhere, he ordered the convert women of Corinth not to speak any more during divine services. At first he had seemed to tolerate the practice in the exceptional case of a woman suddenly endowed with a special gift or charism, but when he came to deal specifically with the question he laid down the principle that, apart from the word "Amen" spoken by all at the end of the ceremonies, women should keep silence in religious gatherings (1 Cor. 11:5; 14:16, 33 ff.). In fact, he had this principle so much at heart that he deemed it advisable to return to it several years later in his First Epistle to Timothy (2:11 f.). In practice, he, too, admitted only men into the ranks of the priests, and appointed only men to teach and direct the faithful in the churches (Acts 14:23; 20:17 ff.; 1 Tim. 3:1 ff.; 5:17 ff.; Tit. 1:5 ff.).

With these reservations, he viewed very favorably the

work that women did in the service of Christianity. We can even say that he sketched out a plan of organization for their activities. Thus it is more likely that the women he mentioned when listing ecclesiastical offices (1 Tim. 3:11) were *deaconesses*, like Phoebe of Cenchrae (Rom. 16:1),[1] rather than the wives of the deacons about whom he had just been speaking. The duties of these deaconesses, which became more specific as time passed, were to assist the poor and the sick, and even the women converts at their baptism. St. Paul seemed to divide the *widows* into two categories— those who helped others and those who received assistance (1 Tim. 5:3–16). He required the older women, whether widowed or not, to train the younger wives by example and counsel so that their domestic virtues might become living sermons (Tit. 2:3 ff.). He accepted Lydia's hospitality (Acts 16:15), approved of the Christian women who helped the Apostles, and informed them about the state of the churches (1 Cor. 1:12; 9:5, Rom. 16:1 f.). He gave the title of his "helper in Christ Jesus" (Rom. 16:3) to the heroic Priscilla, who with her husband, Aquila the tentmaker, completed the religious instruction of Apollos, put her house at the disposal of the faithful, and risked her life to save the Apostle (Acts 18:2 f., 26; 1 Cor. 16:19; Rom. 16:4). With a view to promoting their apostolate, St. Paul put his women readers on guard against their natural tendency toward talking too much, gossiping, dressing expensively, being inquisitive, and giving way to dissipation (1 Tim. 2:9 f.; 3:11; 5:13; 2 Tim. 3:6 f.; Tit. 2:3).

It is therefore false to speak about St. Paul as being a woman-hater: he simply re-stated or elaborated our Lord's own teaching on women. It was the same as regards his teaching on family life. Like Christ, he remained celibate (1 Cor. 7:7 f.; 9:5),[2] and he advised those who had received the necessary grace to do likewise so that they might be able to devote themselves more fully to God's service (1 Cor. 7:7, 25 ff., 34).

But he did not therefore condemn marriage; on the contrary, he regarded as impostors those who would proscribe the sacrament of matrimony, and he recommended it to those of the faithful who had not been granted a higher vocation and even to those young widows who were unable to remain celibate (1 Cor. 7:9, 40; 1 Tim. 5:14). He honored motherhood highly, placing it among the means of salvation (1 Tim. 2:15). He also taught that wives had the same matrimonial rights as husbands (1 Cor. 7:3 ff.), and he did not permit divorce even in the case of separation, which he regarded as a last resort (1 Cor. 7:10 ff.). While he, in his turn, upheld the authority of the husband in the family, he clearly confined that authority to the limits of reason and revelation. In fact, he saw the matrimonial union both as a prefiguring and a re-presentation of the union of Christ with His Church, for he showed that our Lord, in His union with his Church, exercised His authority only for the material and spiritual good of the Church (Ephes. 5:22 ff.; Col. 3:18; 1 Cor. 11:3 ff.). He taught further that, besides wifely obedience in the sense just described, woman's duties included the proper management of her household and the education of her children (1 Tim. 5:14; Tit. 2:3). On the last point he was careful to declare that the mother should not provoke her children, but should raise them by using corrections and reprimands inspired by Christian principles (Ephes. 6:4; Col. 3:21).

Conclusion

What can we conclude from our findings in the New Testament? It is immediately obvious that we see there the confirmation and development of the basic teachings of the Old Testament. We see that woman appears there as a human person in the fullest meaning of the term and that her supernatural destiny is identical with man's. We see that the precise doctrine which we desired on various points was provided there, and needed only to be put into more technical terms, which was done as time passed.

This more precise teaching had a marked effect on the atmosphere of the New Testament. As a result of it, women took their place as men's equals. Of course, in God's providence, which is to a certain extent inscribed in their mental and physical make-up, women cannot take the places that have always been allotted to men in the Church and the family. But they are no longer crushed by men's authority, which was changed from tyranny to benevolence. The New Law is the law of devotion and love (Luke 22:26; John 11:14 ff., 34; Ephes. 5:25 ff.). Hence even the limitations on women's activities that remain, are no longer burdensome. Moreover, at least as regards women's role in family life, these limitations have been greatly reduced by the prospects of a vocation to virginity and by the more humane, Christian concept of the marriage bond.

Furthermore, the part played by the Blessed Virgin, Mother of the Savior and Queen of the Apostles, and, to a lesser degree, that played by Priscilla, St. Paul's "helper," for example, are proof that despite these limitations, women can still have great and irreplaceable roles to fill.

Notes

1. Cf. Pliny the Younger, *Epist.* X, 96.
2. See X. Léon-Dufour's interesting article "Mariage et continence selon S. Paul," in *Mémorial Gelin* (Mappus, 1961), pp. 319–329.

29

Tributes to Our Lady

*Why do the Gospels tell us
so little about Mary?*

"I HAVE ASKED MYSELF," says St. Thomas of Villanova, "why the Evangelists . . . wrote so briefly about the Blessed Virgin's life. . . . Why . . . didn't they tell us anything about her birth, education and habits, about her life . . . with her Son and her relationship with the Apostles after the Ascension . . . ? Why is there not a book entitled *The Acts of the Blessed Virgin* . . . ? I have found only one likely answer —the providence of the Holy Spirit. The Blessed Virgin's glory . . . is completely interior, easier to contemplate than to describe. We know enough about her life when we read that Christ was born of her. What more do you want . . . ? It suffices that she is the Mother of God, for there is no beauty, no virtue, no grace, and no glory that is not reflected in that motherhood.

"The Holy Spirit has not described her in Sacred Writ but has left it to you to visualize her, because He wants you to understand that she lacks no grace, no perfection and no glory that mind can conceive as existing in a mere creature, and, even more, that she surpasses all understanding and thought. Therefore, when everything has been said (about our Lady), it would be useless to go into detail, the more so because, if any item were omitted, we might think that she did not possess it."[1]

The Name of Mary

Nowadays we know that St. Jerome suggested that the name Miryam be translated as *stilla maris*, "sea-drop," and not *stella maris*, "star of the sea," as some copyists read it. St. Bernard knew only the defective translation and elaborated beautifully upon it, but his deductions are valid nevertheless. Here is what he says:

There is indeed a wonderful appropriateness in this comparison of her to a star, because as a star sends out its ray without detriment to itself, so did the Virgin bring forth her Child without injury to her integrity. And as the ray emitted does not diminish the brightness of the star, so neither did the Child born of her tarnish the beauty of Mary's virginity. She is therefore that glorious star, which according to prophecy, arose out of Jacob, whose ray illumines the entire earth, whose splendour shines out conspicuously in heaven and reaches even unto hell; a star which, enlightening the universe, and communicating warmth rather to souls than to bodies, fosters virtue and extinguishes vice. She, I say, is that resplendent and radiant star, placed as a necessary beacon above life's "great and spacious sea," glittering with merits, luminous with examples for our imitation. Oh, whosoever thou art that perceivest thyself during this mortal existence to be rather floating in the treacherous waters, at the mercy of the winds and the waves, than walking secure on the stable earth, turn not away thine eyes from the splendour of this guiding star, unless thou wishest to be submerged by the tempest! When the storms of temptation burst upon thee, when thou seest thyself driven upon the rocks of tribulation, look up at the star, call upon Mary. When buffeted by the billows of pride, or ambition, or hatred, or jealousy, look up at the star, call upon Mary. Should anger, or avarice, or carnal desires violently assail the little vessel of thy soul, look up at the star, call upon Mary. If troubled on account of the heinousness of thy sins, confounded at the filthy state of thy conscience, and terrified at the thought of the awful judgment to come, thou art beginning to sink into the bottomless gulf of sadness and to be absorbed in the abyss of despair, oh, then think of Mary! In dangers, in doubts, in difficulties, think of Mary, call upon Mary. Let not her name depart from thy lips, never suffer it to leave thy heart. And that thou mayest more surely obtain the assistance of her prayer, neglect not to walk in her footsteps.[2]

The Immaculate Conception

In his encyclical *Ineffabilis Deus*, Pius IX gave the basic reason for Mary's Immaculate Conception. He said that it was fitting that she should always shine with the brilliance of the most perfect sanctity; that it was fitting that she should be completely preserved from the stain of original sin, for she was the one to whom God the Father had resolved to give His only Son, whom He had begotten in His own bosom, and to give Him in such a way that He was at once the Son of God and the Son of the Virgin.

Father Sertillanges elaborates as follows on this subject:

We must emphasize the fact that Mary was not placed outside redemption as if she were exempt from it. . . . No, Mary was redeemed by her Son, like all of us. . . . No exception was made for her. Yet she was privileged. When Mary actually became the Mother of Jesus . . . , she was thereby filled with light. Indeed, she was filled with light, in anticipation, from the time of her own conception so that the Son Himself might not be darkened in any way. . . . Others would only be purified: she was completely pure. As Mother of the Day, she would not experience night. He and she were so united that they became one in purity and absolute integrity. It was the springtime of a renewed humanity, the sweet inebriation of the whole world, for although the privilege given to Mary was incomparable and incommunicable, it was not and will not be any the less a treasury for all, in the designs of Providence. Saved by her Son before He was born, Mary is His first trophy of victory and the pledge of all the others. . . . O pure ray of light made into a woman! O smile of the world that in you is delivered from evil and given hope, what a forecast of your holy beauty! You are a cloud of incense that spreads through our atmosphere. . . . Thanks to you, we know here below what the life of the angels is like, and we are no longer ignorant of the graces of Eden.[3]

The Annunciation

In his fourth homily on the praises of the Virgin Mother, St. Bernard (1090–1153) wrote unforgettably about the Annunciation:

O happy Virgin! Thou hast heard what is to be accomplished in thee, and what is to be the mode of accomplishment. Each is a matter for wonder, yet also and equally an occasion of joy. Therefore, "rejoice greatly, shout for joy, O Daughter of Jerusalem," and since "to thy hearing has been given joy and gladness," let us also hear from thee the reply of gladness which we so eagerly long for; and then "the bones that have been humbled shall rejoice." Thou hast heard, I say, what is to be accomplished in thee, and thou hast believed; believe also what has been explained to thee concerning the mode of accomplishment. Thou hast been told that thou shalt conceive and bear a Son: thou has heard that this shall be not by man but by the operation of the Holy Spirit. Behold the Angel now awaits thy answer: "it is time that he should return to the Lord Who sent him." We also, O Lady, await from thy lips the sentence of mercy and compassion, we who are so miserably groaning under the sentence of condemnation. For lo! the price of our salvation is now offered to thee: if thou wilt only consent, we shall at once be set at liberty. We have been created by the eternal Word of God, and behold we die: by thy momentary word we must be renewed and restored to life. O Virgin most loving, Adam, now exiled from Paradise with all his miserable offspring, implores this favor of thee. For this does Abraham entreat thee, for this David, for this all the other holy fathers, thine own ancestors, who are now dwelling in the region of the shadow of death. See, the whole world, prostrate at thy feet, awaits thy answer. And not without cause. For on thy word depend the consolation of the miserable, the redemption of the captives, the pardon of the condemned, the salvation of all the children of Adam, of the entire human race. O Virgin, delay not to answer. Speak the word, O Lady, speak the word which all on earth, and all in limbo, yea, and even all in Paradise are waiting to hear. Christ Himself, the King and Lord of all, longs for thy answer with a longing equal to the ardour wherewith He "hath desired thy beauty," because it is by means of thy consent that He has decreed to save the world. Hitherto thou hast pleased Him by thy silence, but now thy speech shall give Him more pleasure.[4]

Mary's Faith

In her *Novissima Verba,* or "last words," St. Thérèse of Lisieux (1873–1897) spoke at length about the Blessed Virgin's faith:

If a sermon on the Blessed Virgin is to bear fruit, it must show her *real* life, as the Gospel depicts it, and not her *imaginary* life. It is easy to guess that her real life, in Nazareth and later, must have been quite ordinary. . . . "He was subject to them" (Luke 2:51). How simple that is! The Blessed Virgin is sometimes depicted as unapproachable, but she should be shown as one who can be imitated, who practised the hidden virtues, and lived by faith just as we do, as proved by the Gospel, where we read that: "They did not understand the word that he spoke to them" (Luke 2:50), or: "His father and mother were marvelling at the things spoken concerning him" (Luke 2:33). Don't you think . . . that this "marvelling" implies a certain amount of astonishment.[5]

In his book, *The Lord*, Msgr. Romano Guardini also speaks about Mary's faith in striking terms:

"And blessed is she who has believed. . . ." If anything voices Mary's greatness, it is this cry of her cousin Elizabeth. Mary believed blindly. Again and again she had to confirm that belief, and each time with more difficulty. Her faith was greater, more heroic than that of any other human being. . . . More was demanded of Mary than Abraham. . . . Who was this "Holy One" whom she, a mere girl, had borne? This "great" one she had suckled and known in all his helplessness? Later she had to struggle against the pain of seeing him steadily outgrow her love, even purposely flee it to that realm of ineffable remoteness which she could not enter. Not only did she have to accept this, but to rejoice in it as the fulfillment of God's will. Not understanding, never was she to lose heart. . . . Inwardly she accompanied the incomprehensible figure of her son every step of his journey, however dark. . . . This was Mary's inimitable greatness.

And literally, every step the Lord took towards fulfillment of his godly destiny, Mary followed—in bare faith. Comprehension came only with Pentecost. Then she understood all that she had so long reverently stored in her heart. It is this heroic faith which places her irrevocably at Christ's side in the work of redemption, not the miracles of Marianic legend. Legend may delight us with deep and gracious images, but we cannot build our lives on imagery, least of all when the very foundations of our belief begin to totter.[6]

Mary's Divine Maternity

St. Cyril of Alexandria eloquently defended Mary's divine motherhood against Nestorius. Writing shortly before the

Council of Ephesus (431) to the monks of Egypt to put them on their guard against Nestorius's error, he said:

I am astonished that anyone should ask whether or not we should call the Blessed Virgin the Mother of God. For, if our Lord Jesus Christ is God, how could the Virgin who brought Him into the world not be the Mother of God? This is the belief that the holy Apostles handed down to us, even though they did not use that precise title. . . . Furthermore, divinely inspired Scripture declares that the Word of God was made flesh, that is to say, was united to a body endowed with a rational soul. But some may ask, "Is the Blessed Virgin therefore the Mother of the divinity?" To which we reply: The living, subsisting Word was begotten of the very substance of God the Father and exists from all eternity conjointly with Him who begot Him: He is in Him and with Him. But in the course of time He became flesh . . . . He united to Himself a body possessing a rational soul, so that we can say that He was born of a woman according to the flesh. Furthermore, this mystery has a certain analogy with our own birth. In fact, in accordance with the very laws of nature, earthly mothers carry in their wombs the fruits which, obedient to the mysterious powers decreed by God, evolve and finally develop into human form. But it is God who places a soul in each of these little bodies in the way which He alone knows. . . . For the soul is one thing, and the body another. Nevertheless, although the mothers produce only the bodies, we do not hesitate to say that they give birth to the living being, body and soul, and not merely to one of the two elements. . . . Something the same happened at the birth of the Emmanuel. He was begotten of the substance of the Father, being His word, His only-begotten Son; but when He took flesh and became the Son of Man, it is no absurdity to say—rather, it is necessary to confess—that He was born of woman according to the flesh.[7]

The Birth at Bethlehem

The following words were written recently, and although they do not speak of Mary, yet what they say does have value for our daily lives as it had for Mary's:

You (Jesus) are there (in the crib), you who were present at the beginning. . . . You took human form so that we might not lose ourselves in fruitless reasoning. Why then should we go on wandering in the clouds? We longed for what was invisible: now it can be seen. . . . We must have things that are tangible. If we do not have something to touch, we are lost. The Word became flesh, flesh that we can see and touch, as St. John has said. . . . You are not a concept, an abstract notion, an idea . . . , but *someone*, someone alive. There is no longer any temptation to make my God merely human, for He has made Himself man, putting Himself within my reach . . . , (pouring into) my ears and my heart His divine secrets, (making me divine) by His grace. . . . I shall be able to follow you step by step as a child, a youth, a young man, a mature man. I shall meditate upon all your actions and your example, and when you tell me your beatitudes on the mount, I shall understand because they will have been made clear by what I shall have seen . . . your poverty in the wretched stable . . . , your detachment . . . , your obedience and your silence. . . . I shall not rebel when you repeat that if anyone wants to be your disciple, he must at all costs renounce himself and carry the cross, because I shall see you crushed by the Passion . . . , and crucified on Golgotha.[8]

The Purification

In the middle of the seventeenth century, Abbé Santeuil wrote about this mystery:

Open the sacred doors of your Temple, O Sion. Christ, the Priest and Victim, is entering, so let empty images give way to the reality. . . . No longer shall the steaming blood . . . of slaughtered herds be seen, for here God the Son offers Himself on the altars to appease His Father. . . . The Virgin, in whom the hidden divinity has confided . . . , carries in her arms the God whom she brought forth; and she brings young birds, the offering of the poor.[9]

Mary at Nazareth

In his book *Intérieur de Jésus et de Marie*, Père Grou (1731–1803) contemplated Mary's life in Nazareth:

How great Mary seems to me when she commands her Son, not precisely because that Son is God, but because in commanding Him she practises the most admirable virtues, because she commands Him only out of obedience to God's will. . . . Mary led an ordinary life and she was very glad to do so. . . . Revelations and miracles had had their day, which was now past, and she had returned to ordinary routine. . . . No longer did she receive messages from heaven: God no longer raised up Elizabeths, Zacharys or Simeons to tell her of her high destiny. She had become an ordinary village housewife. Her prayer was a prayer of faith and bareness. . . . The other women who (knew) her saw nothing unusual about her.[10]

Calvary

St. Ambrose (340–397) writes:

Mary, the Mother of the Lord, stood beneath her Son's cross, as no less an authority than St. John the Evangelist tells me. Others related how the world had been shaken at the Passion of our Lord, how the sky had been veiled in darkness . . . , how the (good) thief had been received into paradise. But St. John told me . . . how Jesus on the cross had called His Mother. He (St. John) set greater value on this mark of filial devotion offered by Christ to His Mother . . . than on the gift of the kingdom of heaven (to the good thief). Certainly (Christ's) pardoning the thief was a sign of His kindness, but honoring His Mother with such love was much more a sign of His devotion. Behold thy son, He said, Behold thy mother. This was Christ's testament on the cross, dividing the duties of devotion between His Mother and His disciple. Thus our Lord drew up His testament, not merely His public testament, but also His family testament, and St. John, a worthy witness to such a great Testator, signed his name to it. It was a precious testament that left, not money, but eternal life. . . . And Mary . . . awaited, not the death of her beloved Son, but the salvation of the world.[11]

Mary After the Ascension

In his sermon for the feast of the Assumption, 1660, Bossuet tried to describe for us Mary's life after the Ascension:

Night and day, Mary had been engaged in meditating upon God's secret. . . . And did she change her occupation when she had lost her Son? Where do we see her in the Acts of the Apostles or in the tradition of the Church? She is named among those who . . . received the Holy Spirit . . . ; this is what we are told about her. Was not preserving in her heart all that she had seen of her dear Son an employment worthy enough of her? . . . . What (passage from Scripture) does the Church read on the feast of her glorious Assumption? The Gospel account of Mary, the sister of Lazarus, sitting at the Savior's feet and listening to His words (Luke 10:38, 41).[12] Since the Savior's departure, the Church finds nothing more in the treasury of its Scriptures to apply to Mary, Mother of God, and therefore, so to speak, it has borrowed from another Mary the Gospel passage about divine contemplation. What shall we say to those who devise so many beautiful things for the Blessed Virgin? What shall we say, if humble, perfect contemplation is not enough for them? It was enough for Mary and even for Jesus during thirty years; would it not have sufficed for the Blessed Virgin to have continued the practice? Scripture's silence about the Mother of God is . . . more eloquent than any sermon.[13]

The Assumption

In one of his sermons on the glories of Mary Cardinal Newman (1801–1890) points out how fitting was the Assumption:

It was surely fitting . . . , it was becoming, that (Mary) should be taken up into heaven and not lie in the grave till Christ's second coming, who had passed a life of sanctity and of miracle such as hers. All the works of God are in a beautiful harmony; they are carried on to the end as they begin . . . , who can conceive . . . that God should . . . allow the flesh and blood from which (His human body) was taken, to moulder in the grave? Do the sons of men thus deal with their mothers. . . ? Or who can conceive that that virginal frame, which never sinned, was to undergo the death of a sinner? Why should she share the curse of Adam, who had no share in his fall. . . ? She died, then, as we hold, because even our Lord and Savior died. . . . But although she died as well as others, she died not as others die. . . . She was also saved from disease and malady, and all that weakens and decays the bodily frame. . . . She died, but her death was a mere fact, not an effect. . . .[14]

Let us end this long series of quotations with the beautiful words of St. Thérèse of Lisieux:

We all know that the Blessed Virgin is the Queen of heaven and earth, but she is more a mother than a queen, and we should not be led to believe (as I have often heard it said) that, because of her prerogatives, she eclipses the glory of all the saints, just as the sun when it rises makes the stars disappear. How strange that would be! A mother who makes the glory of her children vanish! I think it's quite the opposite. I believe she will greatly increase the splendor of the elect. . . . It's all very well to speak about her prerogatives . . . , but people should be brought to *love* her.[15]

Notes

1. As cited in Regamey, *Les plus beaux textes sur la Vierge Marie* (ed. La Colombe, Paris, 1946) p. 207 f.; Terrien, *La Mère de Dieu*, I, 230 f.
2. "Second Sermon on the Glories of the Virgin Mother," *St. Bernard's Sermons* (Westminster, Maryland: The Carroll Press, 1950) I, 90–92.
3. A. D. Sertillanges, *Mois de Marie* (Ed. du Cerf, Paris), p. 11 f.
4. *St. Bernard's Sermons, op. cit.* I, 123–125.
5. St. Thérèse de Lisieux, *Novissima Verba* (Office central de Sainte-Thérèse, Lisieux), p. 154 f.
6. R. Guardini, *The Lord* (Chicago, H. Regnery, 1954), p. 11 f.
7. As cited in Regamey, *op. cit.*, p. 62 f.; E. Amann, *Le dogme catholique dans les Pères de l'Eglise* (ed. Beauchesne, 1922), p. 332 f.
8. F. Giraudet, *Dans la lumière de Nazareth* (Mignard, Paris), p. 181 ff.
9. Cited in Regamey, *op. cit.*, p. 327.
10. P. Grou, *Intérieur de Jésus et de Marie* (Haton), p. 491 ff.

11. Migne, P. L., 16, 1218 (*Letter to the Clergy of Vercelli*): J. Lebreton, *The Life and Teachings of Jesus Christ Our Lord* (Milwaukee, Bruce, 1935).

12. The Gospel of the new feast of the Assumption is Luke 1:41–50— Elizabeth's words at the Visitation and the first verses of the Magnificat (translator's note).

13. B. Bossuet, *Elévations sur les Mystères* (D. de Brouwer, 1933), p. 692.

14. J. H. Card. Newman, *Discourses addressed to Mixed Congregations* (London, Longmans Green, 1913) p. 370 ff.

15. Cited in Regamey, *op. cit.*, p. 335.

30

Prayers to Our Lady

Prayer of St. Francis de Sales
(1567–1622)

Remember, gentle Virgin, that you are my Mother and that I am your son, that you are powerful and that I am a mere man, weak and sinful.

I beg you, gentle Virgin, to guide me in all my ways and deeds.

Do not say, gracious Virgin, that you cannot, because your beloved Son has given you all power on earth as well as in heaven.

Do not say that you ought not, because you are the Mother of all poor humans and my Mother in particular.

If you were not able to help me, I would excuse you by saying: "It is true that she is my Mother and that she cherishes me like a son, but the poor lady lacks the power and the means to help me."

If you were not my Mother, I would naturally be patient and say: "She is indeed rich enough to help me. But since she is not my Mother, she doesn't love me."

However, gentle Virgin, since you *are* my Mother, and you *are* powerful, how shall I excuse you if you do not come to my relief and do not lend me your help and assistance?

You see, then, Mother, that you have to give me everything I ask for.

For your Son's honor and glory, accept me as your child without regard for my misery and sins. Deliver my soul and body from all evil and give me all your virtues, especially humility. Finally, endow me with all the gifts and graces that please the Holy Trinity, Father, Son, and Holy Spirit. Amen.[1]

Prayer of Fr. Léonce de Grandmaison
(1868–1927)

Holy Mary, Mother of God,
Preserve in me the heart of a child,
Pure and transparent as a spring.
Obtain for me a simple heart
That does not brood over sorrows;
A heart generous in giving itself,
Quick to feel compassion;
A faithful, generous heart that does not forget any favor,
and never holds a grudge for any injury.
Give me a humble gentle heart
Loving without asking any return,
Happy to efface itself
Before your divine Son;
A great, indomitable heart,

That no ingratitude can close,
No indifference can weary;
A heart tortured by its desire for the glory of Jesus Christ,
Pierced by His love
With a wound that will heal only in heaven.

Prayer to Our Lady of Chartres
by Charles Péguy

Star of the sea, behold an ocean of wheat
   And its billowing swell; a cloth beneath the sky
   And the glancing foam, and our granaries piled high
Here you may overlook an ever-spreading sheet. . . .

Star of the morning sky, O Majesty unknown,
   Behold outspread the plain of our poor devotion,
   And behold our heavy sorrow, like an ocean
As we march towards your court and glorious throne. . . .

Sailing to your cathedral city thus we go,
   A rosary of stacks emerges here and there,
   As circular as towers, opulent and rare,
Like forts on a flagship, ringed against the foe. . . .

You see us marching along this highway straight,
   The rain in our teeth, bespattered with mud and dust
   Upon this ample fan opened to every gust,
The broad highway has become our narrow gate. . . .

When we have finished acting our final personage,
   When we have laid down our fantastical array,
   When the mask and cloak at last are thrown away,
Then deign to remember our lengthy pilgrimage. . . .

When in a narrow grave we shall at last be laid
  And after absolution and the requiem Mass,
  Deign to remember this long pilgrimage in Beauce,
O Queen of all vows to whom our vows are made. . . .[2]

The Virgin At Midday[3]
(Paul Claudel)

It is midday. I see the open church. I must go in.
Mother of Christ, I have not come to pray.
I have nothing to offer and nothing to ask.
I have come, Mother, only to gaze upon you.
To gaze upon you, to weep for joy, knowing
That I am your son and that you are there.
For just a moment during which everything stops.
Midday!

To be with you, Mother, in this place where you are.
To say nothing, to gaze upon your face,
To let my heart sing in its own language,
To say nothing but only to sing because my heart is over-
  flowing
Like the blackbird that follows its fancy in sudden strains
  across these skies.
Because you are beautiful, because you are immaculate,
Woman finally restored to grace,
The creature in its first joy and its final flowering.
Ineffably unsullied because you are the Mother of Christ,
Who is Truth in your arms, and the sole Hope, the only
  Fruit.
Because you are the Woman, the Eden of the ancient, for-
  gotten tenderness,
Whose gaze suddenly goes to one's heart and makes the
  gathered tears spring forth.

Notes

1. Cited by Renée Zeller, *Florilège de Notre-Dame* (ed. Flammarion) p. 35 f.

2. Charles Péguy, *The Mystery of the Holy Innocents and Other Poems*, trans. by P. Pakenham (New York, Harper, 1956), p. 22 f., 34. Reprinted by permission of Harper & Row, Publishers, and of Editions Gallimard, Paris, France, publishers of *La Tapisserie de Notre Dame* by Charles Peguy, in which the selection originally appeared under the title, "Presentation de la Beauce a Notre Dame de Chartres." Copyright © Editions Gallimard.

3. *La Vierge à Midi.*

Il est midi. Je vois l'église ouverte. Il faut entrer.
Mère de Jésus-Christ, je ne viens pas prier.
Je n'ai rien à offrir et rien à demander.
Je viens seulement, Mère, pour vous regarder.
Vous regarder, pleurer de bonheur, savoir cela
Que je suis votre fils et que vous êtes là.
Rien que pour un moment pendant que tout s'arrête.
Midi!

Etre avec vous, Marie, en ce lieu où vous êtes.
Ne rien dire, regarder votre visage,
Laisser le coeur chanter dans son propre langage,
Ne rien dire, mais seulement chanter parce qu'on a le coeur trop plein,
Comme le merle qui suit son idée en ces espaces de couplets soudains.
Parce que vous êtes belle, parce que vous êtes immaculée,
La femme dans la Grâce enfin restituée,
La créature dans son bonheur premier et dans son épanouissement final,
Telle qu'elle est sortie de Dieu au matin de sa splendeur originale.
Intacte ineffablement parce que vous êtes la Mère de Jésus-Christ,
Qui est la vérité entre vos bras, et la seule espérance et le seul fruit.
Parce que vous êtes la femme, l'Eden de l'ancienne tendresse oubliée,
Dont le regard trouve le coeur tout à coup et fait jaillir les larmes accumulées. . . .

(Poèmes de Guerre, N.R.F., 1914-15)*

Translated and used here by permission of Editions Gallimard, Paris, France, publishers of *Poèmes de Guerre de Claudel* by Paul Claudel, in which the selection, *La Vierge à Midi,* originally appeared. Copyright © Editions Gallimard.

A NOTE ON THE TYPE

IN WHICH THIS BOOK IS SET

This book is set in Fairfield, a Linotype face, created by Rudolph Ruzicka, distinguished American artist and engraver. Introduced in 1940, Fairfield is almost strictly a book type with much charm and beauty. It is easy to read as one learns from extensive reading since it furnishes some degree of stimulation and pleasure to the eye. The fitting of each letter is practically perfect, which is a real tribute to its designer. This book was composed by Progressive Typographers, Inc., of York, Pa., printed by the Wickersham Printing Company of Lancaster, Pa. and bound by Moore and Company of Baltimore, Md. The typography and design by Howard N. King.